An Appraiser as an Expert Witness

HONDROS
LEARNING™

HONDROS LEARNING™

4140 Executive Parkway

Westerville, Ohio 43081

www.hondroslearning.com

© 2018 by Hondros Learning™. All rights reserved

Published 2018. Printed in the United States of America

20 19 18   1 2 3

978-1-59844-326-4

Note: USPAP references in the course are based on the most recent edition of USPAP.

For more information on, or to purchase, our products, please visit www.hondroslearning.com

Table of Contents

Preface

Many appraisers who are looking for ways to expand their portfolio of services have found that offering expert witness and litigation services can be both rewarding and lucrative. *An Appraiser as an Expert Witness* begins by differentiating the different types of witnesses used in litigation and continues by taking an in-depth look at various Federal rules governing expert testimony. The general civil action process is discussed in detail, including pretrial procedures and what to expect once on the witness stand. Special emphasis explores the appraiser's duties to the professional standards of ethics and competency.

Exam Prep

Additional appraisal products available from Hondros Learning to help students prepare for the licensing exam include the *Appraisal Review Crammer*™, *5th edition*—a valuable self-study or classroom exam preparation guide; and *CompuCram*™ *Appraisal: online Exam Prep* (compucram. com).

About the Contributors

Timothy Detty

Certified General Appraiser, AQB-Certified USPAP Instructor

Timothy Detty has taught thousands of real estate and appraisal students over the course of his teaching career at Hondros College. A practicing Certified General Appraiser, he has also written numerous real estate and appraisal courses and served as both author and expert reviewer for several real estate and appraisal textbooks. In addition to being an AQB-Certified USPAP instructor, Tim is a frequent guest lecturer and contributor to various real estate and appraisal publications and has served as an at-large representative to the Education Council of Appraisal Foundation Sponsors (ECAFS).

Beth Sigg

Certified General Appraiser, AQB-Certified USPAP Instructor

As the owner of Northwest Appraisal Company, Beth has over 14 years of appraisal experience and over 25 years in the real estate business. Beth holds a Certified General Appraisal license in Ohio and Michigan, enabling her to provide appraisals for any type of real estate. Beth also holds an Ohio Real Estate Broker's license.

Witnesses and Their Roles

Key Terms

Condemnation Taking private property for public use through the government's power of eminent domain.

Expert Witness One who provides testimony based on personal knowledge, skill, experience, training, or education. An expert witness is required to meet specific criteria and may testify in the form of an opinion or otherwise.

Fact Witness A party who is reporting factual information about what he or she has seen or heard. There are no opinions expressed by a fact witness.

Federal Rules of Evidence Court rules adopted in 1975 as a means to codify the evidence law applying to the U.S. Federal Courts.

Lay Witness One who is not testifying as an expert witness but may testify beyond the basic factual points permitted by an individual testifying as a fact witness.

Trier of Fact A person, or group of persons, who determines facts in a legal proceeding, usually a trial.

Note: *USPAP definitions & references in the course are based on the most recent edition of USPAP.*

Defining an Expert Witness

Many sources for legal definitions have varying definitions of the term "expert witness." But in general, an **expert witness** is *someone who specializes in a particular topic area and is able to provide opinions without being involved in connection with a particular litigation issue prior to engagement*. Expert witnesses are paid for their work.

Witness v. Expert Witness

There actually is a difference between an appraiser being summoned as a witness and being engaged to be an expert witness. So, before we proceed, let's look at the distinctions between the two roles.

A witness testifying in a role other than that of an expert witness may be labeled as a *general witness*, a *fact witness*, or a *lay witness*. The terms "general witness" and "fact witness" are used by various courts and litigators interchangeably and have no specific reference in most sources of legal definitions, but the term "lay witness" is somewhat different and is directly referenced in the **Federal Rules of Evidence**, which will be discussed later in this chapter.

Fact Witness

A general witness, most often referred to as a **fact witness**, is *a party who is reporting factual information about what he or she has seen or heard*. There are no opinions expressed by a fact witness. An example of an appraiser who has been called as a fact witness might be as follows:

> ## Example
>
> ATTORNEY: Mr. Appraiser, did you perform an appraisal that included an interior examination of the plaintiff's residence on, or about, January 15, 2017?
>
> MR. APPRAISER: Yes, I did.
>
> ATTORNEY: At the time you examined the interior of the property, was the residence furnished?
>
> MR. APPRAISER: Yes, it was.

This example demonstrates the appraiser expressing no opinions and only reporting what he observed on the date of the interior examination of the property. Likely, the appraiser will be paid little, and compensation is often set by the court.

Lay Witness

A **lay witness** is *one who is not testifying as an expert witness but may testify beyond the basic factual points permitted by an individual testifying as a fact witness*. A lay witness may include certain opinions in his testimony; however, the opinions expressed by the lay witness must be:

- Rationally based on the perception of the witness.

- Helpful to the clear understanding of the witness's testimony or to determine a fact in issue.

- Not based on scientific, technical, or other specialized knowledge (such as would be relied upon by an expert witness).

Care must be taken that an individual acting as a lay witness does not venture into the realm of an expert witness, as the Federal Rules of Evidence sets clear expectations for both lay witness testimony and expert witness testimony.

It can be very precarious for professional appraisers to act as lay witnesses since their education and specialized knowledge have the potential to cross the line into the role of expert witnesses. In many cases, a lay witness in testimony involving the value of real property is a non-appraiser, such as a real estate brokerage professional, a builder, an architect, etc., with knowledge of factual value-related data, who expresses an opinion based on the known facts.

Example

Consider a non-appraiser, such as a real estate broker, who is knowledgeable of recent sales prices in the neighborhood of the real property in question. His knowledge would probably not be labeled as specialized as the information is available from public sources (assuming the property is not located in a non-disclosure jurisdiction). Public records indicate a range of sales prices in this neighborhood of $150,000 to $300,000. The attorney asks the broker if $225,000 is a reasonable market value for the subject property. The real estate broker, acting as a lay witness, may state that a market value of $225,000 is reasonable, based upon his perception of the market and his general knowledge of sales prices in the area.

No scientific methodology or technical application of valuation analysis was applied in the real estate broker's opinion, only the broker's perception of the marketplace where testimony of an individual acting as an expert witness would go further.

An appraiser could be a lay witness if the opinion he was expressing was something other than an appraisal or appraisal review—an opinion rendered that did not necessitate applying special methodology, knowledge, or skills.

Example

An appraiser is called upon to provide an opinion of the most common valuation method for a 50-year-old single-family residential dwelling, located in a market that is predominately owner-occupied with sufficient sales activity. The appraiser expresses the opinion that the sales comparison approach is the most reliable for such a property.

The appraiser did not render an opinion that required special methodology, knowledge, or skills. Real estate licensees and many other real estate-related practitioners recognize that the most common method for valuing a property of this type under these circumstances is to rely on comparable sales data.

Expert Witness

Testimony provided by an **expert witness** is *most often based on opinion*, or the expert witness could be helping the **trier of fact** to understand elements of a particular issue.

According to The Federal Rules of Evidence, the expert witness's testimony is based on *knowledge, skill, experience, training, or education* and the expert witness *may testify in the form of an opinion or otherwise if:*

a. *The expert's scientific, technical, or other specialized knowledge will help the trier of fact to understand the evidence or to determine a fact in issue;*

b. *The testimony is based on sufficient facts or data;*

c. *The testimony is the product of reliable principles and methods; and*

d. *The expert has reliably applied the principles and methods to the facts of the case.*

Although the preceding is not exclusive to those testifying in the capacity of an appraiser expert witness as the Federal Rules of Evidence apply to expert witnesses of all fields and specialty skills, the requirements for expert witness testimony are strikingly similar to the often-cited attributes generally possessed by appraisers providing services in context with public trust, which include:

- Specialized knowledge
- Experience
- Impartiality
- Independence
- Integrity

An appraiser providing services as an expert witness must possess these attributes. The obligation to rely on sufficient facts and data, base opinions on reliable principles and methods, and to apply reliable principles and methods is embedded in the development standards of USPAP.

As an expert witness, an appraiser may:

- Provide testimony that merely assists with the court's understanding of how something is to be performed; for example, the steps in the appraisal process, how the scope of work is decided, the process of determining highest and best use, etc.

- Develop and report an opinion regarding an appraisal that has already been performed by another appraiser that is in question—an appraisal review.

- Perform an appraisal of a property that is an element of the matter and provide a report of the findings as part of the testimony.

Federal Rules of Evidence

Now that you've been introduced to the **Federal Rules of Evidence,** let's discuss what these rules are and how they came to be.

The Federal Rules of Evidence was first adopted in 1975 as a means to codify the evidence law applying to the U.S. Federal Courts. Many state and local courts have adopted the Rules, with or without modification. It is likely that states and or jurisdictions create their own rules of evidence that, thus, may or may not be similar to the Federal Rules of Evidence.

The Rules were developed as a regulatory measure for the evidence that may be used to reach a verdict in a litigation matter and give judges great latitude in their ability to admit evidence despite competing arguments from the parties involved. Judges still hold the power to exclude evidence that could unfairly prejudice a party.

Federal Rules of Evidence

The Federal Rules of Evidence consist of 11 Articles and 67 individual rules. The Articles are:

1. General Provisions
2. Judicial Notice
3. Presumptions in Civil Actions and Proceedings
4. Relevancy and Its Limits
5. Privileges
6. Witnesses
7. Opinions and Expert Testimony
8. Hearsay
9. Authentication and Identification
10. Contents of Writings, Recordings, and Photographs
11. Miscellaneous Rules

Note: The 11 articles are numbered in the Federal Rules of Evidence as I through XI and can be accessed online at https://www.rulesofevidence.org.

While an appraiser expert witness is not required to become an expert in formal court rules, being familiar with the rules applicable to expert witness testimony is advisable. Of most relevance to appraisers as an expert witness are the rules found in Article VII, Rules 701 – 706.

Rule 701 and Rule 702

Rule 701 addresses Opinion Testimony of Lay Witnesses and Rule 702 addresses Testimony of Expert Witnesses; portions of these rules were discussed earlier. Let's examine these rules in more detail.

Rule 701 – Opinion Testimony by Lay Witnesses

If a witness is not testifying as an expert, testimony in the form of an opinion is limited to one that is:

    (a) rationally based on the witness's perception;

    (b) helpful to clearly understanding the witness's testimony or to determining a fact in issue; and

    (c) not based on scientific, technical, or other specialized knowledge within the scope of Rule 702.

Source: Federal Rules of Evidence, 2016 Edition, The National Court Rules Committee

Obviously, Rule 701 sets forth the extent to which a lay witness may provide testimony and makes a clear statement that the basis for the testimony cannot be such as to cross over into expert witness testimony as described in Rule 702.

Rule 702 – Testimony by Expert Witnesses

A witness who is qualified as an expert by knowledge, skill, experience, training, or education may testify in the form of an opinion or otherwise if:

(a) the expert's scientific, technical, or other specialized knowledge will help the trier of fact to understand the evidence or to determine a fact in issue;

(b) the testimony is based on sufficient facts or data;

(c) the testimony is the product of reliable principles and methods; and

(d) the expert has reliably applied the principles and methods to the facts of the case.

Source: Federal Rules of Evidence, 2016 Edition, The National Court Rules Committee

Rule 702 clearly defines that an expert witness is relying on his training, education, skills, accepted principles and methodology, and specialized knowledge in the opinions he is expressing in his testimony. As noted earlier, those opinions may be in the form of an appraisal, an appraisal review, or any other opinion developed in the role of an appraiser expert witness.

Rule 703 – Rule 706

The remaining rules contained in Article VII of the Federal Rules of Evidence, Rules 703 – 706, also apply to the appraiser expert witness, in whole or in part. Again, these rules may vary from one state or jurisdiction.

Rule 703 – Bases of an Expert

An expert may base an opinion on facts or data in the case that the expert has been made aware of or personally observed. If experts in the particular field would reasonably rely on those kinds of facts or data in forming an opinion on the subject, they need not be admissible for the opinion to be admitted. But if the facts or data would otherwise be inadmissible, the proponent of the opinion may disclose them to the jury only if their probative value in helping the jury evaluate the opinion substantially outweighs their prejudicial effect.

Source: Federal Rules of Evidence, 2016 Edition, The National Court Rules Committee

Similar to this rule is the SCOPE OF WORK RULE of USPAP, which references the scope of work being acceptable when it meets or exceeds an appraiser's peers' scope of work on a similar assignment.

Rule 704 – Opinion on an Ultimate Issue

*(a) **In General — Not Automatically Objectionable.** An opinion is not objectionable just because it embraces an ultimate issue.*

*(b) **Exception.** In a criminal case, an expert witness must not state an opinion about whether the defendant did or did not have a mental state or condition that constitutes an element of the crime charged or of a defense. Those matters are for the trier of fact alone.*

Source: Federal Rules of Evidence, 2016 Edition, The National Court Rules Committee

The portion of interest to an appraiser in Rule 704 is found in Part (a), which states that *an opinion is not automatically objectionable.* Say, for instance, the appraiser expert witness places the market value of the property in question at $100,000. Just because this opinion of value expressed by the expert witness is consistent with what one party or the other believes does not make it particularly objectionable by the other party.

Rule 705 – Disclosing the Facts or Data Underlying an Expert

Unless the court orders otherwise, an expert may state an opinion — and give the reasons for it — without first testifying to the underlying facts or data. But the expert may be required to disclose those facts or data on cross-examination.

Source: Federal Rules of Evidence, 2016 Edition, The National Court Rules Committee

Rule 705 has significant meaning to an appraiser expert witness. For example, if the opinion of value is premised upon the indications of a sales comparison analysis, the appraiser expert witness may state that the opinion of market value is $100,000 based on the sales comparison approach. The underlying facts or data, such as the specific sales analyzed, the amount of adjustments required, etc., do not have to be included in the expert witness's testimony. However, the expert witness may be required to present these facts or data upon cross-examination.

Rule 706 – Court-Appointed Expert Witnesses

(a) **Appointment Process.** *On a party's motion or on its own, the court may order the parties to show cause why expert witnesses should not be appointed and may ask the parties to submit nominations. The court may appoint any expert that the parties agree on and any of its own choosing. But the court may only appoint someone who consents to act.*

(b) **Expert's Role.** *The court must inform the expert of the expert's duties. The court may do so in writing and have a copy filed with the clerk or may do so orally at a conference in which the parties have an opportunity to participate. The expert:*

    (1) *must advise the parties of any findings the expert makes;*

    (2) *may be deposed by any party;*

    (3) *may be called to testify by the court or any party; and*

    (4) *may be cross-examined by any party, including the party that called the expert.*

(c) **Compensation.** *The expert is entitled to a reasonable compensation, as set by the court. The compensation is payable as follows:*

    (1) *in a criminal case or in a civil case involving just compensation under the Fifth Amendment, from any funds that are provided by law; and*

    (2) *in any other civil case, by the parties in the proportion and at the time that the court directs — and the compensation is then charged like other costs.*

(d) **Disclosing the Appointment to the Jury.** *The court may authorize disclosure to the jury that the court appointed the expert.*

(e) **Parties' Choice of Their Own Experts.** *This rule does not limit a party in calling its own experts.*

Source: Federal Rules of Evidence, 2016 Edition, The National Court Rules Committee

Rule 706 applies when the court appoints an expert witness, either on their own or by motion of one of the parties. The rule makes clear that the expert witness must consent to the appointment. The court must clearly spell out the duties of the expert witness and make the determination of how, and by whom, the expert witness will be paid. The court may allow disclosure to the jury that the court has appointed the expert witness and the parties may still engage their own expert witnesses.

Those Who Hire Appraiser Expert Witnesses and Their Cases

Appraisers who offer expert witness services enjoy an abundance of assignment possibilities. Some potential assignments may require specialized training and expertise while others may require only the appraisal competence already possessed by the appraiser. Competency will be discussed later in this course but now, let's examine various types of cases that often require an appraiser expert witness.

Divorces

Divorce cases may be one of the most common types of circumstances for which an appraiser may provide expert witness services. A typical divorce requires any community property to be divided. If community property includes real property, the services of a real property appraiser are necessary. The court must know the market value of the real property in order to proceed with the division of assets. These cases can be contentious in nature but, given the appraiser has the necessary appraisal competence for common mainstream appraising for the particular type of property involved, do not require specialized skills or knowledge or methodology. However, the effective date of the appraisal may be of particular issue and may vary by case or jurisdiction.

In some cases, the appraiser may have already performed an appraisal of the property, possibly for a different intended use. This scenario and the necessary cautions the appraiser must be aware of will be discussed later in this course. In other cases, the appraiser may be engaged by one of the parties. And perhaps, in rarer instances, the court may have ordered the appraiser to perform an appraisal.

Foreclosures

Not long ago, when the real estate market navigated through some of the toughest times in recent history, many appraisers kept afloat and drew upon assignments of properties connected with foreclosure for survival. The foreclosure process and possible subsequent court cases regarding the establishment of a minimum bid, or a deficiency judgment action, could cause the appraiser to once again become involved either by performing additional appraisals and/or providing expert witness testimony.

Condemnation Actions

Through the power of eminent domain, private property is frequently taken for a public use. The process is known as **condemnation**. Appraisals and appraisal expert witnesses are often an integral part of the process; however, an appraiser contemplating such an assignment must realize that this is one type of expert witness assignment for which specialized competency is required. There are numerous federal and state jurisdictional regulations and statutes that prevail in such assignments. Specialized methodology is also often involved.

Within the expert witness's testimony and any appraisal performed as a preliminary to testimony, the appraiser is not suggesting a particular settlement amount as just compensation. Rather, the appraiser is providing an opinion of the (defined) value of the property portion involved in the taking as well as the effect on any residual portions, if the condemnation is a partial taking. Most often, the appraiser is engaged by the government entity involved in the taking or the property owner to perform an appraisal as well as provide expert witness testimony.

Environmental Contamination

Consider a property that has been contaminated due to toxic run-off from a neighboring property. Litigation frequently follows such damage. Expert witness assignments involving properties that are contaminated are likely to be more complex than those for some other uses:

- In most of the assignments, two appraisals — a before and an after — are necessary.
- Clean-up costs related to remediating the contamination could be an integral element within the valuation process as a cost to cure when ideal data is lacking.
- Expert witness appraisers accepting such an assignment should be intimately familiar with the market reaction to such a property.

Although it's possible the environmental issue can be cured through clean-up, a stigma may remain as the general public is typically skeptical about the clean-up and related issues. It is common for the market to resist properties with known environmental issues. When these properties appear for sale, they may remain on the market for an extended period, possibly resulting in an impact to the value of the property.

The court may rely on the value opinions provided by appraisers to decide a reasonable award for damages due to decreased property value.

Bankruptcy

When a bankruptcy includes real property, an appraisal is usually required. A means test is typically used to determine the type of bankruptcy protection one should file, i.e., Chapter 7 or Chapter 13. The requirements (and means test) may be different in each state.

- All states require the persons or entities filing for bankruptcy to disclose ownership of any and all real property owned.
- Some states require an appraisal indicating the current market value of the real property.
- Even if the state does not require an appraisal by law, many attorneys want an appraisal from a licensed or certified appraiser.

If there is a disagreement regarding the appraiser's value conclusion, the appraiser may be required to make a court appearance. Performing as an expert witness for a bankruptcy proceeding does not typically require any special competency, provided there is nothing unusual about the real property involved.

IRS Matters

Appraisers must be careful when undertaking an appraisal and eventual expert witness assignment for use in an action involving the IRS. Like condemnation work, the IRS has a litany of specific requirements and regulations that must be observed, which can make the assignment somewhat complex. As in many of the potential expert witness assignments discussed, the appraisal is usually performed as of a retrospective effective date.

Real Estate Taxation Disputes

Appraisals are commonly used in real estate tax appeals. Appraisers are often requested to act as an expert witness in a real estate tax disputes as well. The effective date of these assignments is typically retrospective, as of a previous tax lien date.

An appraiser may appear as a witness of fact or as an expert to explain the appraisal and answer questions of a tax appeals board. Permissibility of a third party to be present and speak before a tax appeal panel may vary by jurisdiction.

- In some jurisdictions, an appraiser may be required to appear and present his findings.

- In other jurisdictions, third parties may be prohibited from appearing before the panel.

- For more involved and complex tax appeal issues, the dispute may be elevated to a court of law, in which case, the rules observed by that particular jurisdiction prevail.

Insurance Disputes

Any appraiser who has performed an appraisal for insurance settlements knows the assignment can be brimming with challenges. The assignment might involve a before and after valuation, in which case the property might have been damaged or destroyed and the appraiser is relying upon data, interviews, photographs, public records, etc., for determining the state of the property in its before condition.

- In the case of a structure that has been totally destroyed, such as in a fire, the appraiser may only observe the site and a pile of rubble. The before value is typically expressed as of a retrospective effective date, and obviously, the use of extraordinary assumptions may be necessary.

- Alternatively, the property may be repaired or rebuilt, leaving the appraiser to use other sources for determining the quality and quantity characteristics of the destroyed or damaged structure and its prior-to-loss value.

- In other cases, the repairs or rebuilding may be in suspense awaiting settlement for which the appraiser must determine the finished improvements' value as a prospective value opinion.

Expert witnesses providing services in an insurance settlement dispute case should possess significant support for their conclusions regarding the property in question and the opinions expressed during the process.

Appraisal and Mortgage Fraud Cases

As one could probably imagine, the potential types of cases that could be included in the categories of appraisal fraud and mortgage fraud are broad and various. The court proceedings for these cases may be criminal in nature.

Expert witnesses may be engaged by the defendant, or by a regulatory agency or their counsel, with most cases requiring an appraisal review by the expert witness.

Family and Business Matters

The types of cases involving family or business matters for which an appraiser may be engaged as an expert witness can also run the gamut.

A **partition action** is a common case type where the litigants are business associates or family members.

- In many of these circumstances, one party wants to sell a commonly held property while the other party does not. The court may order the sale and an appraiser is engaged to provide an opinion of value for the property. This appraisal service may lead to expert testimony in court, especially if one of the parties disagrees with the appraiser's value opinion.

- Other types of disagreements, eventually requiring the services of an appraiser expert witness, may be when both parties are willing to sell but can't agree on a selling price. The court may order an independent appraisal be performed, with an eventual appearance by the appraiser as an expert witness.

These cases often arise between family members over inherited property or with business associates when the business entity is closing.

Another common case is when an appraiser is engaged in connection with property owned by a deceased individual, which is being handled by a probate court. The term **probate** means *the proving or authentication of a will*. Probate court is a special court that has the power over the administration of an estate with the purpose to ensure the wishes of the decedent and the estate are carried out. If the estate includes real property, then the services of a real property appraiser may be required. Appearance by the appraiser in probate court is not typical.

Zoning

Most zoning ordinances can be appealed. An appraiser usually comes into the picture during the appeal process. Through examining appraisals, a zoning authority and the general public can determine if a zoning change and/or modification will impact the values of the involved property as well as the properties adjacent. This knowledge assists the zoning board of appeals in making appropriate decisions.

Sometimes, litigation issues arise from these decisions, and an appraiser may able to assist the courts by developing opinions regarding any impact to the value of properties affected by the zoning change. Before and after valuations are typically necessary.

Building Defects and Disputes

Sometimes, builders and contractors perform work that adversely affects a property's value because the work is deficient, unprofessional, and generally below standard, resulting in defects. In circumstances such as this, an appraisal of the real property may reveal if the value was impacted by the work that was completed. A dispute between a former owner and the current homeowner for removing fixtures or causing damage to a property prior to closing or delivery of possession is a prime example of a dispute that could require an appraiser's services.

In these cases, an appraisal to reveal any impact to value of the property is essential.

- For builder quality and building defects, an appraisal of the real property may reveal if the value was diminished by the substandard work that was completed.
- The same value decline can also be measured in cases involving removed fixtures or damage caused by prior owners upon possession delivered to current owners.

When these disputes cannot be arbitrated or settled out of court, litigation often is initiated and the appraiser is likely to be called as an expert witness.

Various Roles of an Expert Witness

For many years, respected appraisal authorities have advised appraisers to develop and report their opinions in such a manner that they could defend their work product in a court of law.

The thought of appearing and speaking before a judge and jury generally produces fear in most appraisers. Appraisers sometimes decline certain appraisal assignments because of their potential to become contentious and for the appraiser to be called upon for a court appearance. Divorces, family and business disputes, condemnation, and tax-related issues are common examples. Even when doing "safe" work, such as appraisals for mortgage lending or certain private appraisal work, the possibility of a future court appearance by the appraiser is not always precluded.

For other appraisers, choosing to provide appraisal services as an expert witness presents an exciting and challenging avenue for appraisal work, which is oftentimes very lucrative.

An appraiser's involvement with litigation can be voluntary or involuntary and may take on different roles in a particular circumstance.

First-Hand Testimony

Providing first-hand court testimony is one of the areas for which an appraiser may be called upon voluntarily or involuntarily. The appraiser may offer fact-based testimony or testimony that includes his professional opinion as an expert witness.

Example

Vic Tory, an appraiser who performed an appraisal for use in a mortgage finance transaction one year ago, is now being called to testify in conjunction with a divorce hearing. He was asked to appear with his workfile and the relevant completed appraisal. He is asked a variety of questions regarding his appraisal.

ATTORNEY: Mr. Tory, did you perform an appraisal of the property in question on or about (one year ago)?

VIC: Yes, I did.

ATTORNEY: Did you conclude an opinion of value of $257,000 in that appraisal?

VIC: Yes.

ATTORNEY: Had a room addition recently been completed to the rear of the home at the time of your appraisal?

VIC: Yes.

Regarding the appraisal he performed, the appraiser, Vic, obviously only confirmed certain facts in providing his first-hand testimony and, therefore, appeared as a fact witness. Usually, this is involuntary and was not anticipated at the time he performed the appraisal.

Alternatively, if the appraiser offers opinions based on his professional expertise, he is considered an expert witness in his first-hand testimony. In this scenario, the appraiser is usually asked to educate the court regarding the methodology used in a particular area of the appraisal process, or even the entire process, and walk the court through the data analyzed and the steps taken to develop his opinions.

Example

The attorney may ask the appraiser to describe the procedure and rationale for various conclusions found throughout a previously completed appraisal report that is now presented as evidence. Let's use the appraiser's opinion of highest and best use as an illustration.

ATTORNEY: In your appraisal report for the property at issue in this case, you concluded that the present use of the property was the property's highest and best use. Is this correct?

APPRAISER: Yes, I did.

ATTORNEY: Can you explain for the court how you arrived at that opinion?

APPRAISER: (Explains the methodology of determining highest and best use)

ATTORNEY: Can you detail the other uses that were considered for the property and why they were eliminated as a potential highest and best use?

The questioning could likely continue to include inquiry regarding the rationale behind the comparable properties selected, how adjustments were derived, methodology for valuing the land, etc. There could even be circumstances in which the appraiser is asked to express an opinion that was not initially developed in the appraisal originally. Care must be taken in this area and will be discussed later in this course.

Another way the appraiser could be called upon as a first-hand expert witness would be when he is specifically engaged by one of the parties involved in the litigation (or possibly the court) to provide an appraisal and subsequent testimony. In these cases, a written appraisal report is usually produced and the testimony provided in the courtroom may extend to an oral appraisal report. Oral reporting will be discussed later in this course.

Appraisal Review Testimony

An expert witness providing an appraisal review as all or part of her engagement is quite common in litigation work. Almost any type of case includes an appraisal review, especially in some particular types of cases, such as mortgage or appraisal fraud.

Commonly, an appraisal completed by another appraiser is at question in such an assignment. The party engaging the appraiser as an expert review witness is either attempting to use the expert witness to affirm the results found in the appraisal being reviewed or to discredit the original appraiser's findings. Of course, as with any appraisal review for any purpose, an expert witness may also perform a review and provide testimony regarding an existing review. As with an expert witness who performs an appraisal and subsequent testimony regarding his opinions and conclusions, an expert witness's testimony that expresses her findings may constitute an oral report.

While the preceding discussion focuses on those times when an appraiser is performing a service for which she is specifically engaged, there may be times in which questioning by either the plaintiff's or defendant's attorney, or even the court, may unintentionally turn to a review. Appraisers acting as expert witnesses must be very cautious of this pitfall.

For example, an expert witness may be under cross-examination by opposing counsel when the attorney produces an appraisal report performed by another appraiser that indicates a vastly different value opinion than that of the expert witness. The interaction might go something like this:

Example

OPPOSING COUNSEL: Ms. Appraiser, you will note that the appraiser performing this appraisal used differing comparable sales than you utilized in your report. Can you explain to the court why the comparable sales you analyzed were better?

APPRAISER: The comparable sales used by the appraiser in this report were not appropriate as they had settled more than a year prior to the effective date and were located several miles from the subject. The sales used in my report were more recent and more geographically similar to the subject property. Also, the appraiser's reconciliation of the sales comparison approach was not adequate as none of the adjusted sales prices bracketed the indicated value by the sales comparison approach, or alternatively, there was no discussion of why the appraiser's opinion of value was outside the range indicated by the adjusted sales prices. <end>

While the appraiser is likely expressing a valid opinion, it expresses the expert witness's opinion regarding the quality of another appraiser's work—an appraisal review. While doing so was most certainly not intentional, it was unwittingly offered by the expert witness who has now placed herself in an uncomfortable position—a review opinion expressed without following the applicable USPAP standards rules for appraisal review development and reporting. More will be discussed on this topic later in this course.

Professional Consultant

There are times when an appraiser may act as an expert and not appear in court. In this role, the appraiser may act as a professional consultant.

- The appraiser may assist one of the parties understanding of the appraisal process, certain methodology, or USPAP compliance requirements.

- It is also possible for a professional consultant to perform an appraisal review of an appraisal that has been presented for his consideration. He may identify questions to be asked and answered during the litigation process, which might bring clarity to something. Or, he might provide additional information that may help in understanding the opinions contained in an appraisal report that is being admitted as evidence.

When acting as a professional consultant, extreme care must be taken that the appraiser does not become an advocate for any party or issue. In compliance with the ETHICS RULE of USPAP, **an individual acting in the role of an appraiser may never advocate**.

- A professional consultant might recommend that the client ask during cross-examination how an adjustment for gross living area was derived, in cases where the methodology for derivation of the adjustment is not clear in the appraisal report. *This is not advocating.* The appraiser is simply saying that it needs more explanation—an explanation that might not benefit nor injure either party's position.

- On the other hand, if the professional consultant recommends that his client only ask questions for which the answer benefits the party he is representing, or assists in developing only cross-examination that benefits his client, *doing such is advocacy*. Advising what to ask and what not to ask is contrary to professional standards.

Advocacy will be discussed in greater detail later in this course.

Chapter Summary

1. A **fact witness** is *a party who is reporting factual information about what he or she has seen or heard*. There are no opinions expressed by a fact witness. A fact witness is typically paid little and compensation is often set by the court.

2. A **lay witness** is *one who is not testifying as an expert witness but may testify beyond the basic factual points permitted by an individual testifying as a fact witness*. A lay witness may include certain opinions in her testimony, but the opinions expressed must be rationally based on the perception of the witness, helpful to the clear understanding of the witness's testimony or to determine a fact in issue, and not based on scientific, technical, or other specialized knowledge.

3. An **expert witness** is *someone who specializes in a particular topic area and is able to provide opinions without being involved in connection with a particular litigation issue, prior to engagement*.

4. Expert witness testimony will be most often based on some type of opinion or helping the **trier of fact** to understand elements of a particular issue. According to the Federal Rules of Evidence, the expert witness's testimony will be based on *knowledge, skill, experience, training, or education*.

5. The **Federal Rules of Evidence** were first adopted in 1975 as *a means to codify the evidence law applying to the U.S. federal courts*. Many states have adopted the rules, with or without modification, as have many local courts.

6. The **Federal Rules of Evidence** were *developed as a regulatory measure for the evidence that may be used to reach a verdict in a litigation matter and to give judges great latitude in their ability to admit evidence despite competing arguments from the parties involved*. Judges still hold the power to exclude evidence that could unfairly prejudice a party.

7. **Rule 701** of the Federal Rules of Evidence addresses **Opinion Testimony of Lay Witnesses**, setting forth the extent to which a lay witness may provide testimony and makes a clear statement that the basis for the testimony cannot be such as to cross over into expert witness testimony as described in Rule 702.

8. **Rule 702** of the Federal Rules of Evidence addresses **Testimony of Expert Witnesses**, clearly defining that an expert witness is relying upon his or her training, education, skills, accepted principles and methodology; and specialized knowledge in the opinions he or she is expressing; and could be in the form of an appraisal, an appraisal review, or any other opinion developed in the role of an appraiser expert witness.

9. **Divorce cases** may be one of the most common types of circumstances for which an appraiser may provide expert witness services. In some cases, the appraiser may have already performed an appraisal of the property, possibly for an intended use other than for use in the divorce litigation.

10. Appraisals and appraisal expert witnesses are often an integral part of the **condemnation process**. This is one type of expert witness assignment for which specialized competency is required.

11. Expert witness assignments involving **contaminated properties** are likely to be more complex than those for some other uses. In most assignments, two appraisals—a before and an after scenario—are necessary.

12. Appraisers must be careful when undertaking an appraisal and eventual expert witness assignment for use in an action involving an **IRS matter**. Like condemnation work, the IRS has a litany of specific requirements and regulations that must be observed, which could make the assignment somewhat complex.

13. Appraisers being called upon to act as an expert witness in a **real estate tax dispute** may also be common in one form or another. The effective date of these assignments is typically retrospective, as of a previous tax lien date.

14. Expert witness work for **insurance settlements** can be very challenging. The assignment might involve a before and after valuation and could require relying upon various sources for determining the state of the property in its "before" condition.

15. Expert witnesses engaged for cases of **appraisal fraud and mortgage fraud** may find the types of cases to be broad and various. With cases of appraisal fraud and mortgage fraud, the court proceedings may be criminal in nature.

16. Types of cases involving **family or business matters** for which an appraiser may be engaged as an expert witness may include partition actions or developing an opinion of value to assist in a buyout of a co-owner's interest(s). With family members, these cases often arise from inherited property. With business associates, the matter is usually associated with the winding down of the business entity.

17. An appraiser's involvement with litigation can be *voluntary or involuntary* and may take on different roles in a particular circumstance.

18. With **first-hand court testimony**, an appraiser may be called upon voluntarily or involuntarily and may offer fact-based testimony or testimony that includes professional opinion as an expert witness.

19. An appraiser may be called voluntarily as a first-hand expert witness when she is specifically engaged by one of the parties involved in the litigation (or possibly the court) to provide an **appraisal and subsequent testimony**.

20. An appraiser may be asked to appear in court, involuntarily, with his workfile and completed appraisal that was previously performed for some other purpose, only to **confirm certain facts** regarding the appraisal that was performed.

21. An expert witness's assignment for almost any type of case could include an **appraisal review**, especially in some particular types of cases, such as mortgage or appraisal fraud, as commonly an appraisal completed by another appraiser is at question in such an assignment.

22. An appraiser may act as an expert and not appear in court. In this role, the appraiser could be acting as a **professional consultant** and extreme care must be taken that the appraiser does not become an advocate for any party or issue.

Chapter Quiz

1. Which type of witness does NOT testify as an expert witness but may testify beyond the basic factual points permitted by someone who testifies as a fact witness?

   A. fact witness

   B. general witness

   C. lay witness

   D. witness for hire

2. Which is a TRUE statement regarding a fact witness?

   A. Fact witnesses can be advocates for a particular party.

   B. No compensation is ever received.

   C. One cannot be a fact witness while in the role of an appraiser.

   D. Opinions are not expressed when acting as a fact witness.

3. Which statement is FALSE regarding the opinions of a lay witness?

   A. All opinions must be based upon scientific, technical, or specialized knowledge.

   B. Lay witnesses and expert witnesses may both offer opinions.

   C. The opinions expressed must be rationally based on the witness's perception.

   D. Opinions must be helpful to the understanding of the testimony or to determine a fact in issue.

4. According to the Federal Rules of Evidence, an expert witness's testimony is based upon

   A. the best interest of the client.

   B. facts and never opinions.

   C. knowledge, skills, training, or education.

   D. subjective conclusions of the witness.

5. What is a typical assignment element of an appraisal performed by an expert witness for a real estate tax dispute case?

   A. before and after scenario

   B. hypothetical condition

   C. jurisdictional exception

   D. retrospective effective date

6. What two types of expert witness assignments may be complex and require special competence due to numerous regulations and specific requirements?

   A. condemnation and IRS matters

   B. family matters and business matters

   C. mortgage fraud and appraisal fraud

   D. tax dispute and divorce

7. What is common regarding assignments involving contaminated property?

   A. appraiser will recommend a settlement award amount

   B. as contaminated, property has no value

   C. EPA certifications will be held by the appraiser

   D. two value opinions will be reported

8. If an appraiser is ordered to court to appear as a witness in a divorce hearing and is asked to bring his workfile for an appraisal he previously completed for a refinance of the property, the appraiser is appearing as

   A. an advocate.

   B. an involuntary witness.

   C. a lay witness.

   D. the trier of fact.

9. When acting in the role of a professional appraisal consultant to a party in a litigation matter, appraisers must take great care to avoid

   A. advising the client on accepted appraisal protocol.

   B. advocating for any party's interest.

   C. expressing technical opinions.

   D. jurisdictional exception being invoked.

10. If an appraiser is engaged by the plaintiff's attorney to provide an appraisal and subsequent oral report for a court case and the parties have agreed upon a fee, the appraiser is acting as

    A. an advocate.

    B. an involuntary lay witness.

    C. the trier of fact.

    D. a voluntary first-hand witness.

Overview of Pretrial Procedures and Rules

Key Terms

Answer Document filed with the court by a defendant in response to a plaintiff's complaint.

Contempt of Court Disrespect for the court or willful disobedience of court rules or orders.

Court Order Directive issued by a judge or court authorizing or requiring the recipient to do, or not do, something.

Daubert Challenge Hearing conducted before a judge where the validity and admissibility of expert testimony are challenged by opposing counsel.

Daubert Standard Provides a rule of evidence regarding the admissibility of expert witnesses' testimony during United States federal legal proceedings.

Defendant Party being sued or accused of a crime in a court of law. In certain cases, called a **Respondent**.

Deponent Person who gives a deposition or affidavit under oath.

Deposition In a lawsuit, the formal, out-of-court testimony of a witness or a party taken before the trial; used as part of the discovery process to determine the facts of the case or when the witness cannot attend the trial.

Discovery, Pretrial Using depositions and interrogatories to learn more about the disputed facts in a case from opposing parties and reluctant witnesses; when each of the opposing parties in a lawsuit is required to disclose requested information and evidence to the other party and each is allowed to examine witnesses who will testify for the other side at trial.

Interrogatories Written questions submitted to the opposing party in a lawsuit during discovery, which the opposing party is required to answer in writing and under oath.

Mediation Process of negotiation by a third party (mediator) to induce an agreement or resolution between parties.

Motion Request for a judge to make a legal ruling.

Motion In Limine Order or ruling limiting or preventing certain evidence from being presented by the opposing party.

Plaintiff Party that brings a case against another in a court of law. In certain cases, called a **Petitioner**.

Pleadings Documents filed with courts stating the position of the parties to a court action.

Summons Document informing a defendant that a lawsuit has been filed against that person or entity and directing the defendant to file an answer to the plaintiff's complaint with the court.

Subpoena Document ordering a person to appear at a deposition or court proceeding to testify or produce documentary or physical evidence.

Subpoena Ad Testificandum Court summons ordering the recipient to appear for testimony in a court of law or other legal authority.

Subpoena Duces Tecum Court order that requires the recipient to appear before the court and produce documents, materials, or other tangible evidence that might be admissible in court.

Voir Dire Legal phrase used to refer to the questioning of a witness or a jury to determine their competence or suitability to testify.

Civil Action Process

In Chapter 1, several types of cases were discussed for which an appraiser may be an expert witness. All presented cases were civil in nature with the exception of the category of mortgage and appraisal fraud, which could be civil but is most often elevated to a criminal issue. In some countries, civil and criminal cases can be combined into one case, but this does not happen in the United States. It should be noted, that there are fundamental differences in procedure between U.S. civil cases and criminal cases. Only the civil action process is discussed in this chapter, as the nuances of criminal prosecution are beyond the scope of this course.

The prospect of being engaged as an expert witness may conjure thoughts of only an appearance in court but, in reality, the role of an expert witness often entails much more than simply providing court testimony. Appraisers who perform work and might be subject to a future court appearance (such as an assignment for a divorce), as well as appraisers who are interested in offering litigation-related services, should be aware of the general procedures of a civil trial. The services of an expert witness may be required prior to a court appearance.

Pretrial Procedures

While an appraiser contemplating being an expert witness may focus mostly on her courtroom testimony, there is actually considerable diligence that takes place before any courtroom event. Portions of the pretrial events may include the participation of the appraiser.

Initiation of Court Action

1. Civil court actions commence with *a party filing a complaint with a court of law*; this party is referred to as the **plaintiff**. The *named party against whom the complaint is filed* is the **defendant**. In some cases, such as a divorce or other domestic dispute, these parties may be referred to as the **petitioner** and the **respondent**, respectively. Within the complaint, the plaintiff recites his view of the facts and the legal basis for the complaint. The complaint asks for certain relief, most commonly monetary damages.

2. The defendant named in the complaint is then notified through the court clerk, by mail or special service (such as a law officer or bailiff), that a complaint has been filed. The method of the notification can vary by jurisdiction. This notice may also be referred to as a **summons** in some jurisdictions.

3. The notice specifies the time period for which the defendant must respond to the complaint with an **answer**. The answer of the defendant typically states why the plaintiff's claims are unfounded, and in some cases, may even prompt a counterclaim by the defendant citing wrongdoing by the plaintiff. Answers, replies to accusations, and counterclaims are common examples of **pleadings**, which are *documents filed with courts stating the position of the parties to a court action*.

4. Parties from both sides of a case file **motions** to request the judge to make a legal ruling. Common examples of motions include:

   - **Motion to dismiss**, saying *the case doesn't have legal grounds* (even though there actually may be grounds)

- **Motion for discovery**, which allows for *the exchange of information between the parties in a case* to reveal the evidence and witnesses that will be presented at trial

Discovery - Preparing for Trial

Once all of the preliminaries are out of the way and the intention of the parties is to proceed with the case to court, the **discovery** process begins. Knowing before the trial what evidence may be presented in court allows each party time to prepare to answer the evidence. Depositions and subpoenas are very common ways that discovery takes place. This is the point where fact witnesses and expert witnesses start to become involved in the trial process.

Depositions and Interrogatories

A **deposition** is *a statement made outside the courtroom, under oath, by each party involved in a case.* The statements made in a deposition can be used in a couple of different ways, at a trial or to prepare for a trial. Certainly, this permits a party to know in advance what a witness will say at the trial. Alternately, a deposition can take the place of oral testimony in court and can be read into evidence at the trial if for some reason a witness cannot personally appear in court. A deposition can be transcribed in writing and/or can be videotaped. While either party can actually take the deposition, both parties have the right to be present.

Just like court testimony, witnesses are deposed orally and then cross-examination can take place by the other side. If the testimony provided by a witness during the deposition differs from the testimony given at trial, an opportunity for the witness to be discredited arises.

As an alternative to oral questioning at depositions, **interrogatories** may be submitted. Interrogatories are *written questions submitted to the other party that are required to be answered in writing under oath.* If one party chooses to use an interrogatory, written questions are sent to the lawyer representing the other side and that party has a period of time in which to answer. Appraisers are sometimes called upon as consultants for composing interrogatories. More on this will be discussed in a later chapter.

Subpoenas and Court Orders

Another way discovery is conducted is by issuing subpoenas to potential witnesses. Knowledge of this process is especially important for appraisers. The terms subpoena and court order are often confused.

- A **court order** is *a directive issued by a judge or court authorizing or requiring the recipient to do, or not do, something.* Court orders must be signed by a judge.

- A **subpoena**, on the other hand, can be issued by an attorney or a court clerk on behalf of the court.

A subpoena is an order to do something and literally means "under penalty." So, if a party receives a subpoena, he must comply with the order or face **contempt of court** penalties, which include potential fines, jail time, or both. Provided the recipient is not one of the parties in the case, the recipient should receive certain compensation for her appearance, which could vary by jurisdiction.

In general, and depending on the jurisdiction, a subpoena is delivered by:

- Personal delivery by a law enforcement officer, an officer of the court, or a civilian process server.
- Certified mail with a return receipt.

The subpoena usually contains:

- Name of the court
- Title of the court case
- Court case number
- Specific commands for which the recipient must comply
- Date of the event or deadline for compliance
- Place of event
- Name of the attorney issuing the subpoena

The term subpoena is most always used generically for the court's command to do something. There are actually two basic types of subpoenas that are commonly used:

- **Subpoena ad testificandum** is *the order of the court to appear for testimony or in a court of law or other legal authority*. For example, when an appraiser is subpoenaed to testify as a fact witness but is not commanded to bring any documentation with her, this is an example of a subpoena ad testificandum.

- **Subpoena duces tecum** is *a court order requiring the production of documents, materials, or other tangible evidence. It is a Latin phrase meaning "You will bring with you under penalty of punishment"*. For example, when the appraiser is ordered to produce and deliver her workfile or to appear in court with the workfile, this is an example of a subpoena duces tecum.

When a subpoena is received, it should be thoroughly read, especially the portions that might note any documentation that should be produced. By virtue of the subpoena:

- The recipient *must appear* and remain at the ordered location until the testimony in the case is closed and excused by the judge. It is helpful to confer at the end of each day of the trial with counsel issuing the subpoena to find out if continued appearance or testimony will be necessary the next day or in the future. Doing so helps to prevent confusion and unnecessary waiting.

- If the party being subpoenaed *does not appear* as the subpoena orders, that individual may be found in contempt of court. In addition to potential fines and jail time, the court may also order the payment of damages because of failure to appear or resistance of discovery. The court may award the opposing party monetary damages that could include lost earnings and reasonable attorney fees.

A party being subpoenaed can request the court to quash (void) or modify a subpoena if it:

- Does not provide a reasonable time period for compliance,
- Presents an undue burden on the individual being subpoenaed, or
- Requires disclosure of confidential or protected information without exception.

No doubt, the last objection citing the required disclosure of confidential or protected information likely resulted in a red flag for appraisers in compliance with the

<u>Confidentiality</u> section of the ETHICS RULE of USPAP. However, it should be remembered that the rule specifically states that *confidential information may be disclosed to third parties as may be authorized by due process of law.* More about confidentiality and appraiser testimony will be discussed in a later chapter.

Any *objections to a subpoena must be made immediately and in writing,* listing all the reasons the recipient feels it is unfair regarding the appearance or production of the requested documents. It may be advisable for the recipient to consult with his or her personal legal counsel regarding objection rights and the appropriate procedure.

Compliance with a subpoena is not a choice! There may be times when there may be serious scheduling conflicts with appearing or complying with the date and time specified in the subpoena. In such cases, the attorney specified in the subpoena may be able to make alternative arrangements. However, if the court date cannot be moved, the individual receiving the subpoena should contact his personal attorney to see if there are any legal avenues for being excused.

Settling or Dismissal Prior to Trial

Before getting too excited about being involved in the procedures and processes of litigation, it should be pointed out that only a very small percentage of cases ever actually make it to trial. There are numerous published statistics that consistently report *90% to 95% of civil cases are settled or dismissed before being heard by a judge.*

Many cases go through some type of an alternative dispute resolution when the case is a dispute between parties. For these types of cases, all 50 states have implemented court rules providing for some use of alternative dispute resolution process. Many jurisdictions go beyond merely offering the possibility and, in some cases, actually *require* the parties to try some other form of alternative dispute resolution. Over half of the states require the use of **mediation** as a pretrial measure in settling disputes.

There are times when the appraiser may be notified in advance of the trial that his appearance is not necessary. But, oftentimes, appraisers who are routinely called upon as a witness, expert, or otherwise may arrive at the courthouse to find that the case has been settled or dismissed. In some cases, this may be after an extended waiting period outside the courtroom.

Several things could cause the litigation process to be settled or dismissed and, in some instances, the appraiser expert witness may have played a vital role. If the expert witness prepared an appraisal for use in the pending litigation, the conclusions of the appraiser may have been the basis for the settlement or dismissal. Or one or more of the parties simply may not have wanted to deal with the stress and time involved in taking the case through the court process. Usually, the reasoning for settling or dismissing is purely economic. Taking a case through the entire process to completion can become very expensive, especially if the position of one of the parties is weak.

 Expert witness fees will be discussed in the last chapter of this course, including compensation while waiting to testify.

Qualifying the Witness

Examination of the qualifying criteria of an expert witness can take place as part of the pretrial procedure, which is usually the case, or during the trial itself. When there is a dispute among the parties of an issue or one party is attempting to prove a point in a legal proceeding, it is safe to say that an expert witness is a very important element in the litigation process.

The extent to which an expert witness is qualified depends on the level of the court in which the issue is being heard as well as the magnitude of the issue. For example, an appraisal expert witness providing services and testimony in a divorce case in a local lower-level court in which the market value of a modest residential dwelling is at issue would certainly be exposed to less qualifying scrutiny than would an expert witness providing services and testimony in a high-level court where the market value of a multi-million-dollar, specialized, industrial facility is at issue.

The qualification criteria for an expert witness may also vary from state to state. Some states have adopted minimum criteria but could also look to higher criteria, such as the Federal Rules of Evidence, which was discussed in Chapter 1.

Role of the Judge

The judge is the "gatekeeper" by which an expert witness and his testimony are qualified as admissible in court.

- In some jurisdictions, an expert witness must be formally accepted before being permitted to offer an opinion or provide testimony.

- Other jurisdictions permit the expert witness to commence his testimony without formal vetting unless the opposing counsel objects and requests the court to provide an opportunity for **voir dire**; in this case, *the questioning of a witness (expert) to determine his or her competence to testify.* (Voir dire can also apply to the questioning of potential jurors to determine their suitability for jury service.)

Whatever the process, the judge, as the gatekeeper, has the responsibility to ensure the witness and testimony are credible. Although the process could vary by jurisdiction, there are certain general qualifying questions that an appraiser expert witness should be prepared for. While not intended to be all-inclusive, the most common questions to anticipate might be:

1. Is property valuation your primary profession?
2. How many years have you been practicing real property appraisal?
3. Do you concentrate upon a particular specialization within the field?
4. What is your specific experience with this type of property?
5. What is your educational background (academic and appraisal-specific)?
6. Do you have a college degree?
7. What is your level of licensure or certification?
8. Are you a member of any professional appraisal organizations?
9. Do you hold any professional certifications or designations?
10. Have you attended or conducted appraisal education courses specific to the property or topic that is the subject of this case?
11. Have you received any awards or other recognition in the appraisal industry?

12. Do you have any published articles regarding appraisal topics?

13. How many cases regarding property valuation or related topics have you been involved in?

The appraiser expert witness should expect additional questions based on her responses to these questions. She should not be offended by these questions. Under cross-examination in complex situations, the probing may become more intense and could turn personal and more deeply rooted. More will be discussed on that topic later.

Daubert Standard

The **Daubert standard** *provides a rule of evidence regarding the admissibility of expert witnesses' testimony during United States federal legal proceedings.* According to this standard, a party may raise a Daubert motion, which is a special case of **motion in limine** (*an order or ruling limiting or preventing certain evidence from being presented by the opposing party*) raised before or during the trial to exclude the presentation of unqualified evidence to the jury.

A **Daubert challenge** is initiated by a Daubert motion and is *a hearing conducted before the judge where the validity and admissibility of expert testimony are challenged by opposing counsel.* The expert is required to demonstrate that her methodology and reasoning are scientifically valid and can be applied to the facts of the case.

The Daubert standard came about as a result of a 1993 court case, *Daubert v. Merrell Dow Pharmaceuticals.* Going back in time, judges have always been the sole gatekeeper of what evidence would be presented and whether it was credible. However, an expert witness who is not actually an expert or who bases her testimony upon atypical or unorthodox methodology or techniques is an injustice to all. Therefore, certain standards have been put in place to ensure quality and credibility. To fully understand the progression of expert witness permissibility and the Daubert standard, one needs to refer to the Frye standard of general witness acceptance.

Frye Standard

The **Frye standard** comes from the 1923 court case of *Frye v. United States*; a case discussing the admissibility of a polygraph test as evidence. The court in Frye held that expert testimony must be based on scientific methods that are sufficiently established and accepted. To meet the Frye standard, *scientific evidence presented to the court must be interpreted by the court as "generally accepted" by a meaningful segment of the associated scientific community.*

From the standpoint of an appraiser, generally accepted by a meaningful segment of the scientific community could refer to the appraisers' peers and recognized methodology typically used throughout the industry. It could also apply to the appraisal process, valuation principles, or techniques that may be presented in a court case.

In the practical application of this standard, the party in a court case who relies on an appraiser using less than mainstream techniques or methodology would be required to provide a number of experts to speak to the validity of the science behind the issue in question. As well, courts were placed in a position necessitating the examination of papers, books, and judicial precedents on the subject at hand to make determinations as to the reliability and "general acceptance."

It should be remembered that the Frye standard is a federal standard for use as an evaluation standard of the acceptability of an expert witness and his testimony; states and lower courts had and still possess the option to adopt it exclusively, or non-exclusively, in whole, or in part. Today, some states still hold to the Frye standard.

Daubert Trilogy

Earlier, it was mentioned that the Daubert standard came about as a result of a 1993 court case of Daubert v. Merrell Dow Pharmaceuticals. There were actually three cases that were an affirmation of the Daubert Standard. These three cases are commonly referred to as the **Daubert Trilogy**.

- *Daubert v. Merrell Dow Pharmaceuticals*, which held in 1993 that Rule 702 of the Federal Rules of Evidence (discussed in Chapter 1) did not incorporate the Frye "general acceptance" test as a basis for assessing the admissibility of scientific expert testimony, but that the rule instead incorporated a flexible reliability standard.

- *General Electric Co. v. Joiner*, which held that a district court judge may exclude expert testimony when there are gaps between the evidence relied on by an expert and his conclusion and that an abuse-of-discretion standard of review is the proper standard for appellate courts to use in reviewing a trial court's decision of whether it should admit expert testimony.

- *Kumho Tire Co. v. Carmichael*, which held in 1999 that the judge's gatekeeping function identified in Daubert applies to all expert testimony, including that which is non-scientific.

Deciding if a particular witness is qualified as an expert can only be accomplished by contrasting the area of the witness's expertise with the subject matter of the witness's testimony. The standard of such review and the criteria for expert witness testimony has been codified by these three cases.

The *Daubert v. Merrell Dow* case cites that Rule 702 does not incorporate the Frye "general acceptance" test as a basis for assessing the admissibility of scientific expert testimony but instead relied upon a flexible standard and was far too liberal.

In Daubert, the Supreme Court ruled that the 1923 Frye test was superseded by the 1975 Federal Rules of Evidence, specifically Rule 702 governing expert testimony. Rule 702 originally stated (in its entirety):

> *If scientific, technical, or other specialized knowledge will assist the trier of fact to understand the evidence or determine a fact in issue, a witness qualified as an expert by knowledge, skill, experience, training, or education may testify thereto in the form of an opinion or otherwise.*

The *Daubert v. Merrell Dow* case makes direct reference to Rule 702 of the Federal Rules of Evidence, which was discussed in Chapter 1. As of this writing, it reads:

> *A witness who is qualified as an expert by knowledge, skill, experience, training, or education may testify in the form of an opinion or otherwise if:*
>
> *(a) the expert's scientific, technical, or other specialized knowledge will help the trier of fact to understand the evidence or to determine a fact in issue;*
>
> *(b) the testimony is based on sufficient facts or data;*
>
> *(c) the testimony is the product of reliable principles and methods; and*

(d) the expert has reliably applied the principles and methods to the facts of the case.

Source: Federal Rules of Evidence, 2016 Edition, The National Court Rules Committee

As can be seen, Rule 702 of the Federal Rules of Evidence has been amended throughout the years to clarify the issues cited in the Daubert trilogy.

Experts are required to provide relevant opinions founded in reliable methodology; those in favor of Daubert were assured that these standards would result in a fair and rational resolution of the scientific and technological issues.

From the standpoint of appraisal expert witnesses, Daubert prevents judges from the necessity of being amateur appraisers and being an "expert" on a topic for which they are not knowledgeable. Daubert creates a *suggested checklist* for which judges can make reasonable determinations regarding the credibility of the witness and the evidence.

1. Has the technique been tested in actual field conditions?

2. Has the technique been subject to peer review and publication?

3. What is the known or potential rate of error?

4. Do standards exist for the control of the technique's operation?

5. Has the technique been generally accepted within the relevant scientific community?

For appraisers, this general criterion prevents an expert witness from applying and promulgating an unacceptable or far-fetched methodology, which typically would not be acceptable to the appraisal community and the appraisers' peers.

The court's gatekeeping function cited in Daubert regarding the admissibility of expert witness testimony was upheld in *General Electric v. Joiner.*

Although the Supreme Court has advised that judges should not use the previously suggested checklist as mandatory (which was a claim in the *Kumho Tire Co. v. Carmichael* case), they can use the checklist as general criteria of acceptability of the expert witness.

Some states have fully embraced the Daubert standard while a few have rejected it completely. Other states have adopted only certain elements. It is important for appraiser expert witnesses to be mindful of the specifications of Daubert as it is likely some or all elements could be a factor in their admissibility as an expert witness.

Federal Rules of Civil Procedure

The **Federal Rules of Civil Procedure (FRCP)** were adopted in 1937 for the purpose of *governing the court procedure for civil cases in United States Federal District Courts.* While the rules apply to practice in all U.S. District Courts, many lower courts also model their procedures and practices to be consistent with the FRCP.

The FRCP consists of 86 rules divided into 11 sections (Titles), plus an Appendix and a section of special purpose rules, and covers the entire litigation process from commencement through final remedies. Not every rule is applicable to expert witnesses and their testimony; however, there are many rules that hold important guidance for expert witnesses.

As with the Federal Rules of Evidence and the Frye and Daubert standards, the applicability of the rules and practice standards may vary by jurisdiction and nature of the trial. Nonetheless, expert witnesses should be somewhat familiar with the content of the various federal rules and procedures. If an appraiser is fairly new to expert witness work, his personal legal counsel is suggested to clarify the exact procedures and rules for the jurisdiction in which he offers expert witness services. If the appraiser expert witness has concerns regarding responsibilities in compliance with the rules applicable in a particular case, consultation with the legal counsel retaining the witness is suggested.

Scope and Purpose of the Federal Rules of Civil Procedure

Rule 1, found in Title I of the Federal Rules of Civil Procedure, is succinct in that the intent of the rules is to streamline the litigation process.

> *These rules govern the procedure in all civil actions and proceedings in the United States district courts, except as stated in Rule 81. They should be construed, administered, and employed by the court and the parties to secure the just, speedy, and inexpensive determination of every action and proceeding.*
>
> *Source: Federal Rules of Civil Procedure, 2016 Edition, The National Court Rules Committee*

 Simply as a point of information, Rule 81, mentioned in Rule 1, recites certain exceptions for the general applicability of the FRCS, none of which would be particularly of interest to an appraiser expert witness.

Several of the subsequent rules also address the efficiency of the process and the timing of events leading to the actual courtroom trial and reinforce the spirit and intent of Rule 1.

 The full Federal Rules of Civil Procedure can be found at https://www.federalrulesofcivilprocedure.org/

Rule 6 – Computing and Extending Time Periods

Rule 6 (in part) addresses how the days or hours specified in any of the rules are to be counted.

> (a) *Computing Time. The following rules apply in computing any time period specified in these rules, in any local rule or court order, or in any statute that does not specify a method of computing time.*
>
> > (1) *Period Stated in Days or a Longer Unit. When the period is stated in **days or a longer unit of time**:*
> >
> > > (A) **exclude the day of the event that triggers** *the period;*
> > >
> > > (B) **count every day**, *including intermediate Saturdays, Sundays, and legal holidays; and*
> > >
> > > (C) **include the last day of the period**, *but if the last day is a Saturday, Sunday, or legal holiday, the period continues to run until the end of the next day that is not a Saturday, Sunday, or legal holiday.*

(2) *Period Stated in Hours. When the period is stated in* **hours**:

   (A) **begin counting immediately on the occurrence of the event that triggers** *the period;*

   (B) **count every hour**, *including hours during intermediate Saturdays, Sundays, and legal holidays; and*

   (C) *if the period would* **end on a Saturday, Sunday, or legal holiday, the period continues to run until the same time on the next day that is not a Saturday, Sunday, or legal holiday**.

Source: Federal Rules of Civil Procedure, 2016 Edition, The National Court Rules Committee

Other parts of Rule 6 address special circumstances, defined legal holidays, and the process for extending time, etc.

Rule 12 - Time to Serve a Responsive Pleading

Rule 12 (in part) details the time limitations for filing a responsive pleading.

   (1) *In General. Unless another time is specified by this rule or a federal statute, the time for serving a responsive pleading is as follows:*

   (A) *A defendant must serve an answer:*

      (i) *within 21 days after being served with the summons and complaint.*

   (B) *A party must serve an answer to a counterclaim or crossclaim within 21 days after being served with the pleading that states the counterclaim or crossclaim.*

   (C) *A party must serve a reply to an answer within 21 days after being served with an order to reply, unless the order specifies a different time.*

Source: Federal Rules of Civil Procedure, 2016 Edition, The National Court Rules Committee

Other parts of Rule 12 address the procedure for presenting a defense, making certain motions, etc. and are directed more to the legal community.

Rule 16 – Purpose of a Pretrial Conference and Sanctions

Rule 16 (in part) recites the purpose of pretrial conferences, such as discovery (submission of written reports from expert witnesses, answers to interrogatories, etc.) and the potential sanctions for attorneys and parties to a case, which would include expert witnesses, for non-compliance. Delivery of written reports and other documents received after the prescribed deadline may not be admissible and the client's case may be lost.

   (a) *Purposes of a Pretrial Conference. In any action, the court may order the attorneys and any unrepresented parties to appear for one or more pretrial conferences for such purposes as:*

   (1) *expediting disposition of the action;*

   (2) *establishing early and continuing control so that the case will not be protracted because of lack of management;*

   (3) *discouraging wasteful pretrial activities;*

   (4) *improving the quality of the trial through more thorough preparation; and*

   (5) *facilitating settlement.*

   (f) *Sanctions.*

   (1) *In General. On motion or on its own,* **the court may issue any just orders, including those authorized by Rule 37(b)(2)(A)(ii)-(vii), if a party or its attorney**:

> *(A) **fails to appear** at a scheduling or other pretrial conference;*
>
> *(B) is substantially **unprepared to participate—or does not participate** in good faith—in the conference; or*
>
> *(C) **fails to obey** a scheduling or other pretrial order.*
>
> *(2) Imposing Fees and Costs. Instead of or in addition to any other sanction, **the court must order the party, its attorney, or both to pay the reasonable expenses—including attorney's fees—incurred because of any noncompliance** with this rule, unless the noncompliance was substantially justified or other circumstances make an award of expenses unjust.*

Source: Federal Rules of Civil Procedure, 2016 Edition, The National Court Rules Committee

Rule 16 is very important to the appraisal expert witness as it addresses the delicate timing for delivery of reports and documents. While extensions of time may be commonplace in other areas of appraisal, such as mortgage lending, such may not be the case in expert witness work with strict regulations. The rule also covers sanctions for non-performance.

Pretrial Disclosure Activities and the Federal Rules of Procedure

There are numerous rules applicable to expert witnesses contained in Title V of the Federal Rules of Civil Procedure titled as *Disclosure and Discovery*, which deserve special attention in this course. Again, state and local courts may have established variations in their own rules. Also, as stated earlier, an appraiser expert witness should seek clarity from legal counsel as to the specific rules applicable in his jurisdiction.

Some of the rules are lengthy, extend beyond the topic of expert witnesses, and are more applicable to the legal community. Therefore, only the applicable portions of the cited rules have been reproduced here and not the rules in their entirety.

Rule 26 – General Provisions and Disclosure Provisions Governing Discovery

Rule 26 of the Federal Rules of Civil Procedure covers disclosure of the identity and contact information of witnesses as well as the location of documents, information, and tangible items possessed by the disclosing party. In general, the rule also addresses the requirement to provide a computation of all damages claimed by the disclosing party. Certain inspection provisions and exemptions from disclosure are also presented.

Portions of Rule 26 are specifically directed to expert witnesses. In fact, if a cursory search is made of the Internet for "Federal Rules of Procedure for Expert Witnesses," the majority of the search results will direct the researcher to Rule 26. Rule 26 is one of the lengthier rules found in the FRCP. Although not all-inclusive, the portions most applicable to expert witnesses are sections 2 and 4 of Rule 26 and are presented here.

> *(2) Disclosure of Expert Testimony.*
>
> *(A) In General. In addition to the disclosures required by Rule 26(a)(1), **a party must disclose to the other parties the identity of any witness it may use at trial** to present evidence under Federal Rule of Evidence 702, 703, or 705.*

As you might recall from the discussion in Chapter 1, Rule 702 of the Federal Rules of Evidence covers *Testimony by Expert Witnesses*. Rule 703 addresses *Bases of an Expert* and Rule 705 discusses *Disclosing the Facts or Data Underlying an Expert*.

> (B) ***Witnesses Who Must Provide a Written Report.*** *Unless otherwise stipulated or ordered by the court,* ***this disclosure must be accompanied by a written report—*** *prepared and signed by the witness—* ***if the witness is one retained or specially employed to provide expert testimony in the case or one whose duties as the party's employee regularly involve giving expert testimony.*** *The report must contain:*
>
> > (i) *a* ***complete statement of all opinions the witness*** *will express and the basis and reasons for them;*
> >
> > (ii) *the* ***facts or data considered by the witness*** *in forming them;*
> >
> > (iii) ***any exhibits*** *that will be used to summarize or support them;*
> >
> > (iv) *the witness's qualifications, including* ***a list of all publications authored in the previous 10 years;***
> >
> > (v) *a* ***list of all other cases*** *in which,* ***during the previous 4 years, the witness testified as an expert at trial or by deposition;*** *and*
> >
> > (vi) *a* ***statement of the compensation to be paid*** *for the study and testimony in the case.*

Obviously, an appraiser expert witnesses whose engagement includes the production of a written appraisal or appraisal review report would be bound by the preceding protocol. Items (i) through (iii) in the list of contents required by the rule directly address the detail and breadth of the written report. The expert witness's rationale and reasoning for her opinions and conclusions must be clearly and completely stated. In most cases, this is accomplished by providing a detailed and compelling narrative within the reconciliation or final summary. The expert witness's report should also include sufficient exhibits and addenda to assist in providing a visual assist in understanding the basis for the appraiser expert witness's opinions and conclusions.

Items (iv) through (vi) of the list are required recitations to be included in an expert witness's written report regarding qualifications and expert witness experience as well as disclosure of the compensation paid to the expert witness. Appraisers often have some type of addenda that is placed in written reports stating their qualifications; in most cases, such an exhibit would suffice or an appraiser could attach a current curriculum vitae or resume. It should be especially noted that the appraiser's addendum of qualifications must include any publications authored within the prior 10 years as well as a listing of all other legal cases in which the appraiser provided expert witness testimony at a trial or deposition within the prior four years. The statement of compensation includes the fees charged for the appraiser expert witness's research, analysis, reporting, and subsequent testimony.

> (C) ***Witnesses Who Do Not Provide a Written Report.*** *Unless otherwise stipulated or ordered by the court, if the witness is not required to provide a written report, this* ***disclosure must state:***
>
> > (i) ***the subject matter on which the witness is expected to present evidence*** *under Federal Rule of Evidence 702, 703, or 705; and*
> >
> > (ii) *a* ***summary of the facts and opinions*** *to which the witness is expected to testify.*

An oral appraisal or appraisal review report presented by an appraiser expert witness may also be appropriate in some cases. Oral reports, as evidenced, have no requirements for presentation of qualifications or experience of the appraiser expert witness nor is there a directive regarding a statement of compensation, as is required in a written report.

> (D) *Time to Disclose Expert Testimony.* **A party must make these disclosures at the times and in the sequence that the court orders.** *Absent a stipulation or a court order, the disclosures must be made:*
>
> > (i) **at least 90 days before the date set for trial** *or for the case to be ready for trial; or*
> >
> > (ii) **if the evidence is intended solely to contradict or rebut evidence** *on the same subject matter identified by another party under Rule 26(a)(2)(B) or (C),* **within 30 days** *after the other party's disclosure.*

There are a couple of important points regarding the timing discussed in part (D) of which an appraiser expert witness must be aware. A written report of the expert witness must be delivered to the opposing party no later than 90 days prior to the date of the trial. Therefore, the expert witness must strictly adhere to the deadlines set by the client. An appraisal review of an appraisal performed by another appraiser engaged by the opposing party must be delivered within 30 days if it will be used in court as a rebuttal.

> (E) *Supplementing the Disclosure. The parties must* **supplement these disclosures when required** *under Rule 26(e).*

If there are items of information or exhibits that are found to be lacking in the appraiser expert witness's original appraisal report, this provision allows for the work to be appended with additional information or for the correction of errors.

> (4) **Trial Preparation: Experts.**
>
> > (A) **Deposition of an Expert Who May Testify. A party may depose any person who has been identified as an expert whose opinions may be presented** *at trial.* **If Rule 26(a)(2)(B) requires a report from the expert, the deposition may be conducted only after the report is provided.**
> >
> > (B) *Trial-Preparation Protection for* **Draft Reports or Disclosures.** *Rules 26(b)(3)(A) and (B)* **protect drafts of any report or disclosure required** *under Rule 26(a)(2), regardless of the form in which the draft is recorded.*
> >
> > (C) **Trial-Preparation Protection for Communications Between a Party's Attorney and Expert Witnesses. Rules 26(b)(3)(A) and (B) protect communications between the party's attorney and any witness required to provide a report** *under Rule 26(a)(2)(B), regardless of the form of the communications,* **except** *to the extent that the communications:*
> >
> > > (i) **relate to compensation** *for the expert's study or testimony;*
> > >
> > > (ii) **identify facts or data that the party's attorney provided and that the expert considered** *in forming the opinions to be expressed; or*
> > >
> > > (iii) **identify assumptions that the party's attorney provided and that the expert relied on** *in forming the opinions to be expressed.*

Part 4 of the rule addresses the nature of the communication between a party's attorney and an expert witness. The rule holds that the appraiser expert witness may be deposed only after providing a report and that draft reports and disclosures are subject to protected confidentiality. As well, the rule specifies that communication between the party's attorney and an expert witness is protected by confidentiality, with the exception of those circumstances referenced in ©, (i)-(iii), which must be disclosed.

> (D) ***Expert Employed Only for Trial Preparation.*** *Ordinarily, a party may not, by interrogatories or deposition, discover facts known or opinions held by an expert who has been retained or specially employed by another party in anticipation of litigation or to prepare for trial and who is not expected to be called as a witness at trial. But **a party may do so only:***
>
> > (i)   *as provided in Rule 35(b); or*
> >
> > (ii) ***on showing exceptional circumstances under which it is impracticable for the party to obtain facts or opinions on the same subject by other means.***

If an expert witness has been engaged as more or less a consultant to assist an attorney during trial preparation and not for the purpose of providing testimony during a trial, there is no duty to disclose any facts or opinions held or expressed by the expert witness, except for under special circumstances. Rule 35(b) referenced in the rule addresses mental and physical examinations, which is not typically an element of a case involving an appraisal expert witness.

> (E) *Payment. Unless manifest injustice would result, the court must require that the party seeking discovery:*
>
> > (i)   *pay the expert a reasonable fee for time spent in responding to discovery under Rule 26(b)(4)(A) or (D); and*
> >
> > (ii) *for discovery under (D), also pay the other party a fair portion of the fees and expenses it reasonably incurred in obtaining the expert's facts and opinions.*

Source: Federal Rules of Civil Procedure, 2016 Edition, The National Court Rules Committee

Part E of the rule makes clear the payment obligations of the party engaging an expert witness to pay the expert witness.

Rule 28 - Persons Before Whom Depositions May Be Taken

Presented here primarily for information purposes, this portion of Rule 28 of the Federal Rules of Civil Procedure describes who may administer oaths prior to a deposition and the definition of an "officer" of the court.

> a) *Within the United States.*
>
> > (1) *In General. Within the United States or a territory or insular possession subject to United States jurisdiction, **a deposition must be taken before**:*
> >
> > > (A) ***an officer authorized to administer oaths*** *either by federal law or by the law in the place of examination; or*
> > >
> > > (B) ***a person appointed by the court*** *where the action is pending to administer oaths and take testimony.*
> >
> > (2) *Definition of "Officer." **The term "officer"** in Rules 30, 31, and 32 includes **a person appointed by the court*** *under this rule or designated by the parties under Rule 29(a).*
>
> (c) *Disqualification. **A deposition must not be taken before a person who is any party's relative, employee, or attorney; who is related to or employed by any party's attorney; or who is financially interested in the action.***

Source: Federal Rules of Civil Procedure, 2016 Edition, The National Court Rules Committee

The portion immediately preceding is of interest as it calls out those interested parties under which a deposition cannot be taken.

Rule 29 - Stipulations About Discovery Procedure

Rule 29 expresses that depositions may take place before any person, any time, and any place. The rule also mandates that any extension of time for the event to take place must have court approval.

Unless the court orders otherwise, the parties may stipulate that:

> *(a) a **deposition may be taken before any person, at any time or place, on any notice, and in the manner specified**—in which event it may be used in the same way as any other deposition; and*

> *(b) other procedures governing or limiting discovery be modified—but **a stipulation extending the time for any form of discovery must have court approval if it would interfere with the time set** for completing discovery, for hearing a motion, or for trial.*

Source: Federal Rules of Civil Procedure, 2016 Edition, The National Court Rules Committee

Rule 30 – Deposition upon Oral Examination

Rule 30 of the Federal Rules of Civil Procedure should be of great interest to expert witnesses. For the most part, the rule specifies the general procedure for which depositions must take place. Only the most relevant portions of the rule are presented here. However, for those relatively new to the world of expert witness work, review of Rule 30 in its entirety would probably be wise.

> *(b) Notice of the Deposition; Other Formal Requirements.*

> > *(1) Notice in General. A party who wants to depose a person by oral questions **must give reasonable written notice** to every other party. The notice must state the **time and place of the deposition and, if known, the deponent's name and address**. If the name is unknown, the notice must provide a general description sufficient to identify the person or the particular class or group to which the person belongs.*

> > *(2) Producing Documents. If a **subpoena duces tecum** is to be served on the deponent, **the materials designated for production, as set out in the subpoena, must be listed** in the notice or in an attachment. The notice to a party deponent may be accompanied by a request under Rule 34 to produce documents and tangible things at the deposition.*

Obviously, the preceding portion of Rule 30 specifies who, where, and when and, if applicable, what items must also be produced at the deposition.

> > *(5) Officer's Duties.*

> > > *(A) Before the Deposition. Unless the parties stipulate otherwise, **a deposition must be conducted before an officer** appointed or designated under Rule 28. The officer must begin the deposition with an **on-the-record statement** that includes:*

> > > > *(i) the **officer's name and business address**;*

> > > > *(ii) the **date, time, and place** of the deposition;*

> > > > *(iii) the **deponent's name**;*

> > > > *(iv) the officer's **administration of the oath or affirmation** to the deponent; and*

> > > > *(v) the **identity of all persons present**.*

You will recall that Rule 28 discussed who may administer an oath at a deposition.

> > > *(B) Conducting the Deposition; Avoiding Distortion. If the deposition is recorded nonstenographically, the officer must repeat the items in Rule 30(b)(5)(A)(i)–(iii) **at the beginning of each unit of the recording medium**. The **deponent's and attorneys' appearance or demeanor must not be distorted** through recording techniques.*

*(C) After the Deposition. At the end of a deposition, the **officer must state on the record that the deposition is complete and must set out any stipulations** made by the attorneys about custody of the transcript or recording and of the exhibits, or about any other pertinent matters.*

The three items specified in item (B) [mentioned in Rule 30 (5) (A)] as necessary to be repeated in a recording at the beginning of each recording unit of the preceding are:

1. Officer's name and business address

2. Date, time, and place of the deposition

3. Deponent's name

In the next section of the rule, examination, cross-examination, and objections are addressed. For the most part, the examination and cross-examination at a deposition are identical to that of a trial.

(c) Examination and Cross-Examination; Record of the Examination; Objections; Written Questions.

*(1) Examination and Cross-Examination. **The examination and cross-examination of a deponent proceed as they would at trial under the Federal Rules of Evidence**, except Rules 103 and 615. After putting the deponent under oath or affirmation, the officer must record the testimony by the method designated under Rule 30(b)(3)(A). The testimony must be recorded by the officer personally or by a person acting in the presence and under the direction of the officer.*

*(2) Objections. An objection at the time of the examination—whether to evidence, to a party's conduct, to the officer's qualifications, to the manner of taking the deposition, or to any other aspect of the deposition—must be noted on the record, but the examination still proceeds; the testimony is taken subject to any objection. An objection must be stated concisely in a nonargumentative and nonsuggestive manner. **A person may instruct a deponent not to answer only when necessary to preserve a privilege, to enforce a limitation ordered by the court, or to present a motion under Rule 30(d)(3).***

In the preceding item 2, the procedure for objections within a deposition is different from the procedure applied in a trial.

*(3) Participating Through Written Questions. Instead of participating in the oral examination, **a party may serve written questions** in a sealed envelope on the party noticing the deposition, who must deliver them to the officer. The officer must **ask the deponent those questions and record the answers verbatim**.*

Written questions are rarely seen used in a deposition.

(d) Duration; Sanction; Motion to Terminate or Limit.

*(1) Duration. Unless otherwise stipulated or ordered by the court, **a deposition is limited to 1 day of 7 hours**. The court must allow additional time consistent with Rule 26(b) (1) and (2) if needed to fairly examine the deponent or if the deponent, another person, or any other circumstance impedes or delays the examination.*

*(2) Sanction. The **court may impose an appropriate sanction**—including the reasonable expenses and attorney's fees incurred by any party—on a person who **impedes, delays, or frustrates** the fair examination of the deponent.*

The point of particular interest in the preceding is the time limit for a deposition. The deposition may not last for more than seven hours per day.

> (e) *Review by the Witness; Changes.*
>
>> (1) *Review; Statement of Changes. On request by the* **deponent or a party before the deposition is completed***, the deponent* **must be allowed 30 days** *after being notified by the officer that the transcript or recording is available in which:*
>>
>>> (A) **to review** *the transcript or recording; and*
>>>
>>> (B) **if there are changes in form or substance, to sign a statement listing the changes and the reasons** *for making them.*
>>
>> (2) *Changes Indicated in the Officer's Certificate. The* **officer must note** *in the certificate prescribed by Rule 30(f)(1)* **whether a review was requested** *and, if so, must* **attach any changes the deponent makes** *during the 30-day period.*

According to section (e) of Rule 30, parties being deposed in a deposition have the right to review the transcript of deposition and make any necessary corrections within 30 days after receiving the transcript. As noted in item (1), the request to review the transcript must be made prior to the conclusion of the deposition.

The remainder of the rule is presented here primarily to illustrate what happens at the conclusion of the deposition.

> (f) *Certification and Delivery; Exhibits; Copies of the Transcript or Recording; Filing.*
>
>> (1) *Certification and Delivery.* **The officer must certify in writing that the witness was duly sworn and that the deposition accurately records the witness's testimony.** *The certificate must accompany the record of the deposition. Unless the court orders otherwise, the officer must seal the deposition in an envelope or package bearing the title of the action and marked "Deposition of [witness's name]" and must promptly send it to the attorney who arranged for the transcript or recording. The attorney must store it under conditions that will protect it against loss, destruction, tampering, or deterioration.*
>>
>> (2) *Documents and Tangible Things.*
>>
>>> (A) *Originals and Copies.* **Documents and tangible things produced for inspection during a deposition must, on a party's request, be marked for identification and attached to the deposition.** *Any party may inspect and copy them. But* **if the person who produced them wants to keep the originals***, the person may:*
>>>
>>>> (i) **offer copies** *to be marked, attached to the deposition, and then used as originals—after giving all parties a fair opportunity to verify the copies by comparing them with the originals; or*
>>>>
>>>> (ii) **give all parties a fair opportunity to inspect and copy the originals** *after they are marked—in which event the originals may be used as if attached to the deposition.*
>>>
>>> (B) *Order Regarding the Originals. Any party may move for an order that the originals be attached to the deposition pending final disposition of the case.*
>>
>> (3) *Copies of the Transcript or Recording. Unless otherwise stipulated or ordered by the court, the officer must retain the stenographic notes of a deposition taken stenographically or a copy of the recording of a deposition taken by another method.* **When paid reasonable charges, the officer must furnish a copy of the transcript or recording to any party or the deponent.**
>>
>> (4) *Notice of Filing. A party who files the deposition must promptly notify all other parties of the filing.*

Source: Federal Rules of Civil Procedure, 2016 Edition, The National Court Rules Committee

Rule 33 - Interrogatories to Parties

As a point of review, interrogatories are written questions submitted to the other party, which they are required to answer in writing under oath. Interrogatories are directed to parties of an action, unlike depositions that question both parties and witnesses. However, as mentioned earlier, an expert witness may be called upon to write interrogatories.

(a) *In General.*

(1) *Number. Unless otherwise stipulated or ordered by the court,* **a party may serve on any other party no more than 25 written interrogatories,** *including all discrete subparts. Leave to serve additional interrogatories may be granted to the extent consistent with Rule 26(b)(1) and (2).*

(2) *Scope. An interrogatory* **may relate to any matter** *that may be inquired into under Rule 26(b).* **An interrogatory is not objectionable merely because it asks for an opinion or contention** *that relates to fact or the application of law to fact, but* **the court may order that the interrogatory need not be answered until designated discovery is complete,** *or until a pretrial conference or some other time.*

(b) *Answers and Objections.*

(1) *Responding Party. The* **interrogatories must be answered:**

(A) **by the party to whom they are directed;** *or*

(B) *if that party is a public or private corporation, a partnership, an association, or a governmental agency, by any* **officer or agent,** *who must furnish the information available to the party.*

(2) *Time to Respond.* **The responding party must serve its answers and any objections within 30 days after being served with the interrogatories.** *A shorter or longer time may be stipulated to under Rule 29 or be ordered by the court.*

(3) *Answering Each Interrogatory. Each interrogatory must, to the extent it is not objected to, be* **answered separately and fully in writing under oath.**

(4) *Objections.* **The grounds for objecting to an interrogatory must be stated with specificity.** *Any ground not stated in a timely objection is waived unless the court, for good cause, excuses the failure.*

(5) *Signature.* **The person who makes the answers must sign them,** *and the attorney who objects must sign any objections.*

Source: Federal Rules of Civil Procedure, 2016 Edition, The National Court Rules Committee

Rule 34 – Production of Items of Evidence and Entering onto Land for Inspection, Etc.

Portions of Rule 34 are especially important and applicable to appraiser expert witnesses.

(a) *In General.* **A party may serve on any other party a request** *within the scope of Rule 26(b):*

(1) *to produce and permit the requesting party or its representative to inspect, copy, test, or sample the following items in the responding party's possession, custody, or control:*

(A) **any designated documents or electronically stored information**—*including writings, drawings, graphs, charts, photographs, sound recordings, images, and other data or data compilations—stored in any medium from which information can be obtained either directly or, if necessary, after translation by the responding party into a reasonably usable form; or*

(B) *any designated tangible things; or*

(2) ***to permit entry onto designated land or other property possessed or controlled by the responding party, so that the requesting party may inspect, measure, survey, photograph, test, or sample the property*** *or any designated object or operation on it.*

Source: Federal Rules of Civil Procedure, 2016 Edition, The National Court Rules Committee

Needless to say, the preceding addresses the accessibility to a workfile. This section of the rule also provides clarity regarding the inspection of the property by an expert witness.

Chapter Summary

1. Civil court actions commence with a **plaintiff** filing a complaint with a court of law. The named party against whom the complaint is filed is the **defendant**. In some cases, such as a divorce or other domestic dispute, these parties may be referred to as the **petitioner** and the **respondent**, respectively.

2. The defendant named in the complaint is notified through the court clerk by mail or special service that a complaint has been filed. The notice may be referred to as a **summons** in some jurisdictions. It specifies the time period for which the defendant must respond to the complaint with an **answer**. Answers, replies to accusations, and counterclaims are common examples of **pleadings**.

3. Parties from both sides of a case file **motions** to *request the judge to make a legal ruling*. A **motion to dismiss** means the case doesn't have legal grounds (even though there actually may be grounds). A **motion for discovery** allows for the *exchange of information between the parties* in a case to reveal the evidence and witnesses that will be presented at trial.

4. A **deposition** is *a statement made outside the courtroom, under oath, by each party involved in a case.* If a witness cannot personally appear in court, a deposition can take the place of oral testimony in court and can be read into evidence at the trial. A deposition can be transcribed in writing, videotaped, or both. While either party can take the deposition, both parties have the right to be present during the deposition.

5. As an alternative to oral questioning at depositions, **interrogatories** may be submitted. Interrogatories are *written questions, submitted to the other party, which they are required to answer in writing under oath.*

6. Another way discovery is conducted is by issuing **subpoenas** to potential witnesses. A subpoena is an order to do something and literally means "under penalty." Two basic types of subpoenas that are commonly used: **Subpoena ad testificandum** is *the order of the court to appear for testimony or in a court of law or other legal authority*; and **subpoena duces tecum** is *a court order requiring the production of documents, materials, or other tangible evidence.* Any objections to a subpoena must be made *immediately and in writing*, listing all the reasons the recipient feels it is unfair regarding the appearance or production of the requested documents.

7. A **court order** is *a directive issued by a judge or court authorizing or requiring the recipient to do, or not do, something.*

8. **Contempt of court** is *disrespect for the court or willful disobedience of court rules or orders.* A party who does not comply with a subpoena or a court order may face contempt of court penalties, which include potential fines, jail time, or both.

9. Numerous published statistics report that **90% to 95%** of civil cases are settled or dismissed before being heard by a judge.

10. Some jurisdictions permit the expert witness to commence testimony without formal vetting unless the opposing counsel objects and requests the court provide an opportunity for **voir dire**, *the questioning of a witness to determine the witness's competence to testify.* Voir dire could also mean *the questioning of potential jurors to determine their suitability for jury service.*

11. The **Daubert standard** comes from the 1993 court case of *Daubert v. Merrell Dow Pharmaceuticals*. This standard provides a rule of evidence regarding the *admissibility of expert witnesses' testimony during United States federal legal proceedings*.

12. A Daubert motion is a special case of **motion in limine** (an order or ruling limiting or preventing certain evidence from being presented by the opposing party at the trial of the case) raised before or during the trial to exclude the presentation of unqualified evidence to the jury. A **Daubert challenge** is initiated by a Daubert motion and is a hearing conducted before the judge where the validity and admissibility of expert testimony are challenged by opposing counsel.

13. The **Daubert Trilogy** comprises three court cases: Daubert v. Merrell Dow Pharmaceuticals, General Electric Co. v. Joiner, and Kumho Tire Co. v. Carmichael. Daubert creates a *suggested checklist* for which judges can make reasonable determinations regarding the credibility of the witness and the evidence.

14. The **Frye standard** comes from the 1923 court case of *Frye v. United States*, which discusses the admissibility of a polygraph test as evidence. To meet the Frye standard, *scientific evidence presented to the court must be interpreted by the court as "generally accepted" by a meaningful segment of the associated scientific community*.

15. The **Federal Rules of Civil Procedure (FRCP)** *govern the court procedure for civil cases in United States Federal District Courts*.

16. **Rule 1** states the intent of the FRCP is to *streamline the litigation process*.

17. **Rule 6** (in part) addresses *how the days or hours specified in any of the rules are to be counted*.

18. **Rule 12** (in part) details the *time limitations for filing a responsive pleading*.

19. **Rule 16** (in part) recites the *purpose of pretrial conferences,* such as discovery (submission of written reports from expert witnesses, answers to interrogatories, etc.) and the *potential sanctions* for attorneys and parties to a case, which include expert witnesses, for non-compliance.

20. **Rule 26** covers *disclosure of the identity and contact information of witnesses, as well as the location of documents, information, and tangible items possessed by the disclosing party*.

21. **Rule 28** describes *who may administer oaths prior to a deposition and the definition of an "officer"* of the court.

22. **Rule 29** expresses that *depositions may take place before any person, any time, and any place.* The rule also mandates that any extension of time for the event to take place must have court approval.

23. **Rule 30** primarily *specifies the general procedure for which depositions must take place*.

24. **Rule 33** provides the *process for interrogatories.* A party may serve up to 25 interrogatories on the other party, which can be a person.

25. **Rule 34** provides *details on producing documents, electronically stored information, and tangible things or entering onto land for inspection and other purposes*.

Chapter Quiz

1. What is a formal, out-of-court testimony of a witness or party taken under oath before the trial?
    A. answer
    B. deposition
    C. motion
    D. pleading

2. Which statement regarding a deposition is FALSE?
    A. Both parties in a case may be present during the deposition.
    B. A deposition can be transcribed in writing or videotaped.
    C. A deposition can take the place of oral testimony in court.
    D. A deposition does not require the parties to be under oath.

3. The discovery phase of a case
    A. allows the exchange of information between the parties.
    B. allows the pleadings for each party to be filed in the court.
    C. enables interrogatories to be submitted to the judge.
    D. permits each party the time to question all witnesses in a case.

4. Written questions that are submitted to the opposing party in a lawsuit during discovery are called
    A. depositions.
    B. interrogatories.
    C. pleadings.
    D. summons.

5. An order presented to an appraiser to testify as a fact witness and produce his workfile is an example of a(n)
    A. interrogatory.
    B. pleading.
    C. subpoena ad testificandum.
    D. subpoena duces tecum.

6. Typically, what percentage of civil cases are settled or dismissed before being heard by a judge?
    A. 20-25%
    B. 50-55%
    C. 70-75%
    D. 90-95%

7. Which provides a rule of evidence regarding the admissibility of expert witnesses' testimony during United States federal legal proceedings?
    A. Daubert challenge
    B. Daubert motion
    C. Daubert standard
    D. Daubert trilogy

8. Rule 6 of the Federal Rules of Civil Procedure addresses how to count the days and hours specified in the rules. Identify the statement that is TRUE regarding Rule 6.
    A. When the period is stated in days or a longer unit of time, count every day excluding intermediate Saturdays, Sundays, and legal holidays.
    B. When the period is stated in days or a longer unit of time, exclude the day of the event that triggers the period.
    C. When the period is stated in hours, begin counting 24 hours after the occurrence of the event that triggers the period.
    D. When the period is stated in hours, count every hour excluding hours during intermediate Saturdays, Sundays, and legal holidays.

9. An expert witness has requested to review the transcript of a deposition he will be providing. How many days must be allowed for him to review it once the officer notifies him that the transcript is available?
    A. 5
    B. 10
    C. 20
    D. 30

10. Which statement about interrogatories is FALSE?
    A. Each interrogatory must be answered separately and fully in writing under oath.
    B. Interrogatories cannot be served to a public or private organization.
    C. A party may serve a maximum of 25 interrogatories.
    D. The person who answers the interrogatories must sign them.

Expert Witnesses and Appraiser Professional Standards

3

Key Terms

Appraisal Practice Valuation services performed by an individual acting as an appraiser, including but not limited to appraisal and appraisal review.

Appraisal Review The act or process of developing an opinion about the quality of another appraiser's work that was performed as part of an appraisal or appraisal review assignment; (adjective) of or pertaining to an opinion about the quality of another appraiser's work that was performed as part of an appraisal or appraisal review assignment.

Assignment a valuation service that is provided by an appraiser as a consequence of an agreement with a client.

Assignment results Appraiser's opinion or conclusions developed specific to an assignment.

Bias Preference or inclination that precludes an appraiser's impartiality, independence, or objectivity in an assignment.

Confidential Information According to USPAP standards, information that is 1) Identified by the client as confidential when providing it to an appraiser and is not available from any other source. 2) Classified as confidential or private by applicable law or regulation.

Credible Worthy of belief.

Jurisdictional Exception Assignment condition established by applicable law or regulation which precludes an appraiser from complying with a part of USPAP.

Scope of Work Type and extent of research and analyses in an appraisal or appraisal review assignment.

True Copy Replica of an entire written report transmitted to the client, created by photocopy or an electronic copy.

Valuation Services Services pertaining to aspects of property value.

Workfile Documentation necessary to support an appraiser's analyses, opinions, and conclusions.

Appraiser Expert Witness Compliance

While an appraiser expert witness is responsible for compliance with the legal and courtroom pretrial procedures, he is not expected to be a first-hand expert in the legal field. The court or attorney engaging the expert witness will assist in guiding him through the legal process, but compliance with USPAP and appraisal best practices before and during a court event is the responsibility of the appraiser performing as an expert witness.

Accurately executing these practices is important because:

- The work of an expert witness is frequently reviewed for non-compliance.
- Non-compliance with appraisal professional standards is a frequent disqualifier.
- Courts and attorneys may not be knowledgeable of appraisal standards and inadvertently direct the expert witness to violate those standards.
- Attorneys may try to discredit the expert witness through consultation with another expert witness.
- An expert witness may need to comply with appraisal standards not typically at issue in traditional appraisal work.

Opposition's Goal - Make the Witness Appear Inept

It is unlikely the appraiser expert witness's unbiased testimony and any supporting work products would better support the opposition's position. In that event, the party engaging the appraiser expert witness would have already relieved him of his duties. That is certainly the client's option provided, of course, payment for services was not contingent upon the appraiser expert witness's results being favorable to the client's position.

The most common goal of the appraiser expert witness is to present an unbiased and independent testimony that is contrary to the point of view and goals of the opposition. Unless the stakes are low, the opposition will likely work diligently to discredit the expert witness. If the expert witness is unprepared and the opposing counsel is successful in their attempts to make him appear inept, the appraiser expert witness could lose all credibility and potentially leave embarrassed.

USPAP Knowledge as Defense

Attorneys are most often not scholars of USPAP and appraisal best practices any more than an appraiser expert witness is an authority on the Federal Rules of Civil Procedure. However, the opposition can and will engage parties who are authorities on USPAP to assist them in determining compliance with USPAP and appraisal best practices. Opposing attorneys frequently hire appraisers as consultants and reviewers regarding USPAP compliance and application of best practices.

An expert witness who fails to comply and is not knowledgeable of USPAP will be silenced. However, an appraiser expert witness who has applied best practices and observed professional standards can successfully defend her actions with knowledge of USPAP.

Expert Witnesses are on Their Own

An expert witness must serve as his own compliance and professional standards compass. He may be asked to comment or express an opinion that can be seen as inappropriate, or premature, in light of professional standards.

For example, the attorney engaging the expert witness, without notice, asks for his opinion of an appraisal report presented by opposing counsel and performed by another appraiser. That question might be recognized as a request to *express an opinion about the quality of another appraiser's work*, which is actually an appraisal review. If the expert witness responds to that question without performing the diligence required in an appraisal review assignment, he violates professional standards.

In the example above, the question placing the expert witness in an uncomfortable situation came from the attorney *engaging* the appraiser as an expert witness. Remember, **the engaging attorney does not represent the appraiser expert witness**. Each expert witness is on his own with compliance of appraisal professional standards and accepted best practice. The appraiser must rely on his familiarity with USPAP to quickly recognize that the question cannot be answered at that particular time through the request of the attorney without due appraisal review development and reporting diligence.

 *Important Point:* It is **always recommended that appraisers have their own legal counsel** available for consultation on such issues.

Expert Witnesses and USPAP Rules

An expert witness must be thoroughly familiar with the fundamental rules of USPAP to avoid non-compliance and to work with professional standards. Non-compliance is often cited as a reason to discredit an expert witness. However, certain portions of the rules are more prominent and meaningful in expert witness work. It is critical that appraisers undertaking an expert witness assignment recognize how USPAP Rules apply to any type of assignment.

Ethical Responsibilities

Violations of professional ethics are the leading cause of disciplinary actions against appraisers. These same violations are also likely primary reasons why appraiser expert witnesses are discredited.

- The appraiser's actions, or inactions, might be simple, innocent, and unintended. Nevertheless, the appraiser must vigilantly comply with ethical standards.

- In expert witness work, the appraiser may face ethical issues not typically noticed or challenged in traditional appraisal work. Remember, the opposition often actively looks for some ethical indiscretion to discredit the appraiser expert witness.

The ETHICS RULE of USPAP sets forth foundational obligations when acting in the role of an appraiser and amplifies that an appraiser is required to always observe the highest standards of professional ethics.

Inherent within this requirement are general obligations for an appraiser to:

- **Not misrepresent his role when providing a valuation service that is outside of appraisal practice** – *the valuation services performed by an individual acting as an appraiser*;

- Perform in compliance with USPAP when required by law, regulation or agreement;

- Certify compliance with USPAP; and

- Not communicate in a manner that is misleading.

The ETHICS RULE is applicable to an appraiser's conduct, in general, as well as to development and communication issues.

*An appraiser **must** comply with USPAP when obligated by law or regulation, or by agreement with the client or intended users. In addition to these requirements, an individual **should** comply any time that individual represents that he or she is performing the service as an appraiser.*

While all these general provisions of the ETHICS RULE are important in appraiser expert witness work, the obligation to *not misrepresent one's role when performing a service outside of appraisal practice* is emphasized. Sometimes, there can be confusion when providing an expert witness or consulting assignment regarding whether the individual providing the service is acting in the role of an appraiser.

Some might argue that if the individual is assisting legal counsel as a consultant in developing interrogatories, etc., that individual is not acting as an appraiser. Possibly not, but the individual must ask the following:

- Was I engaged because of my appraisal expertise?

- Is the client expecting me to act as an appraiser?

- Am I representing myself as an appraiser?

- Am I using my appraisal expertise in this assignment?

If the answer to any of those questions is "yes", the service is appraisal practice. If the answer is "no", the service is a valuation service outside of appraisal practice and the individual must not misrepresent that role.

Legal counsel engaging the appraiser may suggest that the individual does not need to act in the role of an appraiser in any case. However, **compliance is the responsibility of the appraiser, regardless of what any other party might suggest.** The significance of this will become much clearer as we discuss conduct issues. Portions of USPAP Advisory Opinion 21 are helpful to understand this potentially sensitive situation.

ADVICE FROM THE ASB ON THE ISSUE: #7

What are the USPAP obligations for valuation services outside of appraisal practice?

> *…many individuals have other professional roles in addition to their appraiser role. For example, some appraisers are also attorneys, accountants, brokers, or consultants. USPAP also places an obligation on an individual who sometimes acts as an appraiser even when he or she provides a valuation service in some other capacity – that obligation being not to mislead the users of the valuation service about the capacity in which he or she is acting. The ETHICS RULE states that an appraiser must not misrepresent his or her role when providing valuation*

services that are outside of appraisal practice. If a valuation service is premised on advocacy or compensation arrangements that are contrary to the ETHICS RULE, the valuation service is not consistent with the objectives of USPAP and cannot be performed by the individual acting as an appraiser.

An individual who sometimes provides services as an appraiser but who is currently acting in another role, must ensure that intended users are not misled as to the individual's role in providing that valuation service. This can be accomplished through such means as disclosure, notification, or careful distinction when providing the valuation service as to the individual's role. Additionally, clear representation of the valuation services to be rendered in the engagement communication, scope of work description, or contract, as well as in written and oral correspondence with the client, should assist in ensuring intended users are not misled.

USPAP ADVISORY OPINION 21: Illustration 4

Litigation Services

4. Marie Vaughn has a diverse practice with a specialization in litigation services. She commonly aids attorneys in developing cross-examination strategies for expert witness testimony from appraisers. How does USPAP apply to Marie's "litigation services?"

> *Answer: In order to determine Marie's obligation, it is necessary to understand the nature of her role. If she is acting as an appraiser, her litigation services are part of appraisal practice. The DEFINITIONS, the PREAMBLE, the ETHICS RULE, the COMPETENCY RULE, and the JURISDICTIONAL EXCEPTION RULE will apply to the assignment. As an appraiser, Marie cannot act as an advocate for any party or issue.*
>
> *If Marie's services include providing an opinion of value, she must also comply with the appropriate appraisal standards (STANDARDS 1 and 2, 7 and 8, or 9 and 10). If Marie's services include providing an opinion about the quality of another appraiser's work, the appraisal review requirements of STANDARDS 3 and 4 apply. If the service includes providing analysis, recommendation, or an opinion to solve a problem where an opinion of value is a component of the analysis leading to the assignment results, then Marie must comply with the ETHICS RULE, the COMPETENCY RULE and the JURISDICTIONAL EXCEPTION RULE for the entire assignment; and she must also comply with any applicable Rules and Standards if she performs an appraisal or appraisal review as part of the assignment.*
>
> *On the other hand, if Marie provides litigation services as an advocate, then she is providing a valuation service outside of appraisal practice. When performing services outside of appraisal practice, Marie can act as an advocate and accept contingent compensation. The only USPAP obligation is that she not misrepresent her role. She must use care to distinguish her role from other roles that would carry an expectation of being impartial, objective, and independent, i.e., acting as an appraiser.*
>
> *Marie may provide litigation services by either acting as an appraiser or acting as an advocate for the client's cause; however, she must not perform both roles in the same case.*

Conduct Issues

There are several areas of conduct referenced in appraisal professional standards that are especially applicable to an expert witness assignment:

- Independence
- Bias
- Advocacy
- Required disclosures

Failure to comply with professional standards in these areas is especially delicate for an appraiser expert witness. Non-compliance can be simple to detect by an opposing counsel seeking to discredit the appraiser expert witness.

Obligations of the <u>Conduct</u> section of the ETHICS RULE regarding general conduct include:

- *Appraisers must not engage in criminal conduct*
- *Appraisers must always be impartial, objective, and independent, without accommodating personal interests*
- *Appraisers must perform in compliance with USPAP*
- *Appraisers must not willfully or knowingly violate the requirements of the RECORD KEEPING RULE*

Examine each of the highlighted rules in more detail.

Avoid Criminal Conduct

An appraiser expert witness must not engage in criminal conduct. For an appraiser expert witness, this includes perjuring oneself on the witness stand by being untruthful.

Maintain Impartiality

An expert witness must always be impartial. It can be very easy to become overly involved in doing a good job for the engaging party's side and gravitate toward partiality. Unless the appraiser is vigilant of this obligation, he may be easily led toward the interests of the engaging party by the engaging side's attorney. This is because expert witnesses from other fields and professions may not be obligated to remain impartial in their role.

In some cases, advocacy for their client's position may be required. For example, an expert witness who is a real estate broker typically has the fiduciary duty to the client to act in the client's best interest. Retaining counsel may need to be educated or reminded that appraisers must remain impartial in compliance with professional ethics.

Record Keeping Obligations

An expert witness has record keeping obligations for any **workfile**, when applicable, just as an appraiser has in mainstream appraisal work. When the record keeping obligations of the expert witness are deliberately not in compliance, that action (or inaction) becomes a violation of the ETHICS RULE.

Ethical Obligations

The <u>Conduct</u> section of ETHICS RULE continues with an appraiser's ethical obligations regarding development issues by stating:

- *Appraisers must not perform an assignment with bias.*
- *Appraisers must not advocate for the cause or interest of any party or issue.*
- *Appraisers must not accept assignments that include reporting predetermined opinions and conclusions*
- *Appraisers must not misrepresent their role when providing valuation services outside of appraisal practice.*
- *Appraisers must not perform assignments in a grossly negligent manner.*

Perform Without Bias and Avocation

The expert witness's obligation to remain unbiased and not advocate for any party's position is indirectly referenced in the <u>Conduct</u> section of the ETHICS RULE. The direct reference to the prohibition of bias and advocacy is clear.

Accepting Assignments

The Conduct section of ETHICS RULE prohibits individuals acting as an appraiser to accept an assignment that includes reporting predetermined opinions and conclusions. Obviously, this action by an expert witness would equate to a lack of independence, as well as bias and advocacy.

Specific examples of an assignment with unacceptable conditions that an appraiser expert witness may not accept are cited in the <u>Management</u> section of the ETHICS RULE.

Communicating Assignment Results

The <u>Conduct</u> section of ETHICS RULE prohibits communicating assignment results with the intent to mislead or defraud. This portion of the rule states (in part):

Appraisers must not:

- *Use or communicate a report or assignment results known by the appraiser to be misleading or fraudulent.*
- *Knowingly permit an employee or other person to communicate a report or assignment results that are misleading or fraudulent.*

The ethical obligation for an appraiser to not allow others to use a fraudulent or misleading report can arise in an appraiser expert witness or consulting service.

Scenario

An appraiser has been engaged as a consultant by an attorney to assist in preparing interrogatories for a case involving real property. The attorney is relying on the appraisal prepared for the property owner by another appraiser. While the role of the appraiser as a consultant is not that of a reviewer and no review has been performed by him of the existing appraisal, he has read the appraisal. He has also driven by the subject property and referenced the property's tax records. The appraiser consultant immediately recognizes the photos in the appraisal report are not photos of the subject property. Certain elements regarding the property improvements reflected in the tax records are dissimilar to what was reported in the appraisal report.

Scenario (cont.)

Because of these issues, the appraisal appears to be misleading, if not fraudulent. It is the obligation of the appraiser consultant to advise the attorney, engaging him to not rely on the report.

Note: The appraiser consultant was not developing opinions regarding the appraisal presented to him. He was stating that the data reported did not match the characteristics of the property, which was a matter of fact.

The ethical obligation to disclose current or prospective interests and any prior services before accepting an assignment (or during an assignment) require that the following information must be disclosed to the client:

- **Current or prospective interest in a subject property or the parties involved in the assignment**

- **Services as an appraiser, or in any other capacity, regarding the subject property performed within a three-year period immediately preceding acceptance of the assignment**

The comment to this portion of the <u>Conduct</u> section of the ETHICS RULE provides specific advice regarding how these requirements interact with the appraiser's obligation of confidentiality:

> <u>Comment</u>: *Disclosing the fact that the appraiser has previously appraised the property is permitted except in the case when an appraiser has agreed with the client to keep the mere occurrence of a prior assignment confidential. If an appraiser has agreed with a client not to disclose that he or she has appraised a property, the appraiser must decline all subsequent assignments that fall within the three-year period.*
>
> ***In assignments in which there is no appraisal or appraisal review report, only the initial disclosure to the client is required.***

If the appraiser who is offered the opportunity to perform as an expert witness or consultant has any relationship or interest with the parties or the property involved, the appraiser must decline. These circumstances disqualify the appraiser from participating and are contrary to the rules and regulations of evidence and civil procedure.

Scenario

Scenario 1

An appraiser has been asked to be an expert witness regarding a property he previously appraised two years ago. He is not preparing a new appraisal for the expert witness assignment. At the time of the appraisal assignment, appearing as an expert witness was not within the scope of work. The expert witness assignment is a new assignment and disclosure of the prior assignment is required before accepting the assignment. Since no certification is required for the expert witness assignment, the initial disclosure is all that is necessary.

Scenario (cont.)

Scenario 2

An appraiser has been asked to perform an appraisal of a property involved in litigation, and to appear as an expert witness in a future court procedure where he will provide an oral report. The appraiser has not provided a prior service in the three years prior to acceptance of the assignment. In this case, the appraisal and the expert witness service are all part of the same assignment and the only disclosure is that no applicable prior service has been performed in the oral report certification. <end>

Management Issues

While there are a variety of topics addressed in the <u>Management</u> section of the ETHICS RULE, the most pertinent to an expert witness assignment is the prohibition of accepting an assignment with unacceptable assignment conditions.

The <u>Management</u> section of the ETHICS RULE states, in part:

An appraiser must not accept an assignment, or have a compensation arrangement for an assignment, that is contingent on any of the following:

- *the reporting of a predetermined result (e.g., opinion of value);*
- ***a direction in assignment results that favors the cause of the client;***
- *the amount of a value opinion;*
- ***the attainment of a stipulated result (e.g., that the loan closes, or taxes are reduced); or***
- ***the occurrence of a subsequent event directly related to the appraiser's opinions and specific to the assignment's purpose.***

Mainstream appraisers should be familiar with this portion of the ETHICS RULE. In traditional appraisal, most are aware that the client cannot propose a reduced fee, or pay no fee, if the value desired (or needed) is not met. In litigation work, similar compensation scenarios may be proposed for, let's say, when the engaging party wins the case. Such would be an example of an assignment that is *contingent on a subsequent event* and, thus, an unacceptable assignment condition.

Confidentiality Issues

Most appraisers are aware of the sensitivity of protecting information that is confidential and the parties to which the information can be disclosed without the consent of the client. For appraisers performing work primarily for the mortgage lending industry, the provision of providing an appraisal report to the borrower or having discussions regarding confidential elements or assignment results is prohibited. In expert witness work, other confidentiality issues arise that are not typically seen in mainstream appraisal work.

The <u>Confidentiality</u> section of the ETHICS RULE reviews terms about confidential information from the USPAP DEFINITIONS:

CONFIDENTIAL INFORMATION: *information that is either:*

- *Identified by the client as confidential when providing it to an appraiser and is not available from any other source.*
- *Classified as confidential or private by applicable law or regulation.*

The <u>Confidentiality</u> section of the ETHICS RULE addresses, in part:

- Protection of the confidential nature of the appraiser-client relationship.

- Acting in good faith with the legitimate interests of the client relating to confidential information and in communicating assignment results.

- Fulfilling the obligation to be aware and to comply with all confidentiality laws and regulations applicable to an assignment.

- Defining disclosure requirements and exceptions to the protection of confidential information and assignment results.

    *An appraiser must not disclose **(1) confidential information; or (2) assignment results** to anyone other than:*

    - *the client;*

    - *parties specifically authorized by the client;*

    - *state appraiser regulatory agencies;*

    - ***third parties as may be authorized by due process of law**; or*

    - *a duly authorized professional peer review committee except when such disclosure to a committee would violate applicable law or regulation.*

The non-disclosure provision within USPAP includes both confidential information and assignment results. The USPAP definition of assignment results must also be reviewed.

ASSIGNMENT RESULTS: *An appraiser's opinions or conclusions developed specific to an assignment.*

<u>Comment</u>: *Assignment results include an appraiser's:*

- *opinions or conclusions developed in an appraisal assignment, not limited to value;*

- *opinions or conclusions, developed in an appraisal review assignment, not limited to an opinion about the quality of another appraiser's work; or*

- *opinions or conclusions developed when performing a valuation service other than an appraisal or appraisal review assignment.*

Physical characteristics are not assignment results.

Per the USPAP, an **assignment result** is *any opinion or conclusion developed by an appraiser in an appraisal or appraisal review, or in a valuation service that does not include an appraisal or appraisal review.* Assignment results are not limited to only the appraiser's value opinion or review opinion.

The <u>Confidentiality</u> section of the ETHICS RULE discusses disclosure of confidential information and assignment results to *third parties as may be authorized by due process of law*, without the consent of the client.

Who are the third parties and what is the due process of law referenced in this portion of the rule?

Most commonly, third parties are the attorney from either side of a case or the judge. The due process is a court order or a subpoena. A judge might also demand disclosure of confidential information and assignment results from an appraiser who is testifying as a witness. But, an attorney requesting disclosure or delivery of documents, such as a copy of a report from a prior assignment or the workfile from a prior assignment, does not have that authority without authorization in the form of a court order or subpoena. In such cases, the appraiser does not need to be defiant, but explain an obligation to professional standards and offer to cooperate once the attorney produces the appropriate authorization.

A USPAP FAQ titled ***Due Process Under Confidentiality*** assists in understanding the issue:

> ***Question: I received a request from my state attorney general's office to turn over some appraisal reports I had prepared. Can I comply with this simple request or must it be in the form of a subpoena?***
>
> ***Response:*** *The <u>Confidentiality</u> section of the ETHICS RULE states, in part:*
>
> *An appraiser must not disclose: (1) confidential information or (2) assignment results to anyone other than:*
>
> - *the client;*
> - *parties specifically authorized by the client;*
> - *state appraiser regulatory agencies;*
> - *third parties as may be authorized by due process of law; or*
> - *a duly authorized professional peer review committee except when such disclosure to a committee would violate applicable law or regulation.*
>
> *USPAP does not identify what constitutes due process of law. While a subpoena or court order might clearly constitute due process, a simple verbal or written request might not. Therefore, for requests of this type, it may be necessary to seek legal counsel to determine what constitutes due process.*

Record Keeping Obligations

The RECORD KEEPING RULE of USPAP is applicable when the appraiser expert witness provides an appraisal or appraisal review as part of the duties of the assignment. The following workfile obligations are noteworthy:

- Extra care must be taken that the appraiser's workfile for the assignment is complete.
- A workfile is not required for other services provided in connection with a litigation assignment, including consulting with an attorney for developing interrogatories.
- Essential obligations are the content requirements of the workfile and those regarding its custody and retention.
- An appraiser must prepare a workfile for each appraisal or appraisal review assignment.
- A workfile must be in existence prior to the issuance of any report.
- A written summary of an oral report must be added to the workfile within a reasonable time after the issuance of the oral report.

Oral reports are not usually common in mainstream appraisal work; however, since many appraisal and appraisal review reports include an oral report given as testimony for appraiser expert witness work, the obligation regarding the written summary of the oral report must be noted.

According to the RECORD KEEPING RULE:

The workfile must include:

- *the name of the client and the identity, by name or type, of any other intended users;*

- *true copies of all written reports, documented on any type of media. (A true copy is a replica of the report transmitted to the client. A photocopy or an electronic copy of the entire report transmitted to the client satisfies the requirement of a true copy);*

- ***summaries of all oral reports or testimony, or a transcript of testimony, including the appraiser's signed and dated certification;***

- *all other data, information, and documentation necessary to support the appraiser's opinions and conclusions and to show compliance with USPAP, or references to the location(s) of such other data, information, and documentation; and*

A workfile in support of a Restricted Appraisal Report or an oral appraisal report must be sufficient for the appraiser to produce an Appraisal Report. A workfile in support of an oral appraisal review report must be sufficient for the appraiser to produce an Appraisal Review Report

The workfile for an oral appraisal or appraisal review report (or testimony) must include either a summary of what was orally reported or a transcript of the testimony, which should be available from the court. The workfile must also contain a signed and dated certification for oral reports.

Custody of a Workfile

There may be occasions when the appraiser expert witness is testifying regarding an appraisal performed in the past or has been ordered to produce the report or workfile for a prior appraisal. It could be possible that the workfile is in the custody of another; possibly a co-appraiser or maybe an appraisal firm with which the appraiser expert witness was previously affiliated. The following portion of the RECORD KEEPING RULE addresses such a situation:

An appraiser having custody of a workfile must allow other appraisers with workfile obligations related to an assignment appropriate access and retrieval for the purpose of:

- *submission to state appraiser regulatory agencies;*

- ***compliance with due process of law;***

- *submission to a duly authorized professional peer review committee; or*

- *compliance with retrieval arrangements.*

<u>***Comment:***</u> ***A workfile must be made available by the appraiser when required by a state appraiser regulatory agency or due process of law.***

An appraiser who willfully or knowingly fails to comply with the obligations of this RECORD KEEPING RULE is in violation of the ETHICS RULE.

In the scenario previously presented, the party (co-appraiser or former affiliated company) having custody of the workfile MUST allow the appraiser needing to comply with the due process of law access to the workfile. Ignoring the obligation and refusing to allow access to the workfile is a violation of the ETHICS RULE.

Minimum Retention Period

Finally, an appraiser testifying in an assignment about a prior appraisal or appraisal review could change the minimum retention period for a workfile. Per the RECORD KEEPING RULE:

*An appraiser must retain the workfile for a period of at least five years after preparation **or at least two years after final disposition of any judicial proceeding in which the appraiser provided testimony** related to the assignment, whichever period expires last.*

 Note that *final disposition* means completely finished and settled. An appraiser expert witness may have provided testimony in a case that was subsequently appealed one or more times. The final disposition occurs at the conclusion of the final appeal. In such case, the minimum retention period could be many years.

Scenario

Let's look at two scenarios for how this obligation can be applied:

Scenario 1

An appraiser expert witness performs an appraisal and provides testimony all within the same year in a court case. The case was finally disposed at the conclusion of the hearing and there were no appeals. The minimum retention period is five years after he prepared his report.

Scenario 2

An appraiser expert witness has been engaged to provide testimony about an appraisal he performed four years prior. Final disposition of the case was on the same day as the appraiser expert witness's testimony. In this case, the workfile must be retained for a minimum of two years from the date of the final disposition. Hence, the minimum workfile retention period is about six years.

USPAP FAQs Regarding Workfiles for Court

There are several USPAP FAQs that address a workfile when there has been testimony in court by an appraiser, including:

Question: Is a transcript of an oral report or testimony required for the workfile when an appraiser testifies about an appraisal assignment?

Response: No. There is no absolute requirement to have a transcript of the appraisal oral report testimony. The RECORD KEEPING RULE requirement is for the workfile to contain summaries (which are typically prepared by the appraiser) or a transcript. In cases where summaries are retained, a transcript is not required.

Question: Does the requirement to have a transcript or summary of testimony apply if the appraiser has a written appraisal report and testifies only to the information contained in that report?

Response: Yes. A transcript or summary of the testimony must be included in the workfile when the appraiser testifies about a written report. While the report that is the subject of the appraiser's testimony must also be included in the assignment workfile, it does not replace a summary of the testimony.

Question: Does the requirement to have a transcript or a summary of the appraiser's testimony apply only in assignments when an appraiser provides an oral report?

Response: No. The requirements identified in the RECORD KEEPING RULE apply to both oral reports and testimony in an appraisal or appraisal review assignment.

Question: If an appraiser prepares a written appraisal report, is the workfile required to contain a separate signed certification for any testimony the appraiser provided in support of that report?

Response: In cases where testimony is provided about information contained in a written appraisal report or appraisal review report, a signed certification is required to be included in the written report. The requirement to include a signed certification is satisfied by including a true copy of the report in the workfile, consistent with the RECORD KEEPING RULE.

Question: Must the workfile contain a transcript or summary of an appraiser's testimony for the entire proceeding, or only for that portion that contains the appraiser's testimony?

Response: The appraiser's workfile must contain a summary or a transcript of the appraiser's testimony in an appraisal or appraisal review assignment. The appraiser is not obligated to retain summaries or transcripts for other segments of the proceedings in which testimony was provided by individuals other than the appraiser.

Competency Obligations

An appraiser expert witness can expect that his knowledge will be fully vetted. In some cases, significant examination and cross-examination may take place to prove or support an expert witness's competency. Competency obligations were included in the federal court rules and procedures discussed in an earlier chapter (number of cases in which testimony, published authored works, etc.)

According to the COMPETENCY RULE of USPAP, competency may apply to the appraiser's knowledge and experience regarding:

- *A specific type of property or asset.*
- *A market.*
- *A geographic area.*
- *An intended use.*
- ***Specific laws and regulations.***
- *An analytical method.*

An expert witness's experience in these areas will be closely scrutinized.

Competency Related to Specific Laws and Regulations

A specific area of concern is competency pertaining to specific laws and regulations. This may vary by the type of litigation (tax appeals (IRS) and cases involving condemnation, federal bankruptcy, etc.) having different regulations than those typically found in a mainstream appraisal.

Components of the COMPETENCY RULE include, in part:

- *Possessing competency prior to accepting an assignment.*
- *Having the ability to identify the problem.*
- *Having knowledge and experience to competently complete the assignment.*
- *Recognizing and complying with pertinent laws and regulations.*
- *Recognizing when an appraiser lacks competency.*

The COMPETENCY RULE also provides for the appraiser to disclose the lack of knowledge or experience before agreeing to accept an assignment, or if facts discovered during an assignment reveal a lack of competency. However, in almost every case, if the appraiser expert witness does not possess the required competency prior to agreeing to accept the assignment, the appraiser should decline the expert witness opportunity, as the expert witness would likely be disqualified prior to testifying.

Scope of Work Obligations

Most appraisers are well-acquainted with the SCOPE OF WORK RULE of USPAP. For the expert witness, there are a few areas of the rule that are important to note. The RECORD KEEPING RULE and the SCOPE OF WORK RULE are only applicable in an appraisal or appraisal review connected within an expert witness assignment. An appraiser acting as a consultant, or in a similar role, and not performing an appraisal or appraisal review has no scope of work obligations.

USPAP defines **SCOPE OF WORK** as: *the type and extent of research and analyses in an appraisal or appraisal review assignment.*

The SCOPE OF WORK RULE addresses three primary obligations for appraisers in an appraisal or appraisal review assignment. In an applicable expert witness assignment, each of the following areas are important:

- Problem Identification
- Scope of Work Acceptability
- Disclosure Obligations

Problem Identification

The appraiser has an obligation to ensure that the problem has been properly identified. In this process, the appraiser must identify various elements, including conditions that affect the scope of work and laws and regulations applicable to the assignment. For expert witness work, these laws and regulations could be different than those applicable in many common assignments. USPAP provides guidance about these laws and regulations:

- *Laws include constitutions, legislative and court-made law, administrative rules, and ordinances.*
- *Regulations include rules or orders, having legal force, issued by an administrative agency.*

The SCOPE OF WORK RULE, in part:

- Establishes fundamental considerations by the appraiser in determining the proper scope of work in an assignment.

- Requires the appraiser to properly identify the problem and gather and analyze information about the assignment elements that lead the appraiser to a scope of work decision.
- Describes the role of the client in determining the scope of work in an assignment.
- Establishes a benchmark for scope of work acceptability.
- Discusses the disclosure obligations of the appraiser regarding the scope of work performed in an assignment.

In general, when an appraiser determines the appropriate scope of work to be applied in an assignment, a decision is made regarding (but not limited to) the:

- Extent to which a property is identified.
- Extent of property inspection (tangible property).
- Type of data to be researched and to what extent.
- Type and extent of analysis applied to reach opinions or conclusions.

USPAP recognizes that these elements will not be the same in every assignment, or with every property.

The SCOPE OF WORK RULE requires that the scope of work be determined by each appraisal or appraisal review assignment.

Lenders and others who are intended users of traditional appraisal work may set a minimum scope of work to be performed and the appraiser can expand that scope. It is the appraiser's obligation to ensure the scope of work is appropriate and sufficient to yield assignment results that are credible or *worthy of belief.*

In expert witness work, the engaging party (usually an attorney) may also prescribe the scope of work. One of the cautions regarding the scope of work as an expert witness is that the appropriateness of the appraiser's scope of work may be more closely scrutinized. Remember, the expert witness's entire appraisal process could be reviewed by an appraiser secured by the opposition. Appraisers in traditional assignments are probably less likely to experience this type of scrutiny by their intended users.

The SCOPE OF WORK RULE goes on to say:

Credible assignment results require support by relevant evidence and logic.

The credibility of assignment results is always measured in the context of the intended use.

Very often, the scope of work necessary for the intended use is greater than that found in traditional appraisal assignments. Since the term "credible" is used so often in context to the appraiser's obligations, the USPAP definition of the term should be reviewed:

CREDIBLE: *worthy of belief.*

Scope of Work Acceptability

The second section of the SCOPE OF WORK RULE, Scope of Work Acceptability, addresses the acceptability of the scope of work in an assignment and commences with a general obligation:

- *The scope of work must include the research and analyses that are necessary to develop credible assignment results.*

The comment following this obligation defines how the appraiser determines when the scope of work in an assignment is accepted.

In part, the <u>Comment</u> states:

The scope of work is acceptable when it meets or exceeds:

- *the expectations of parties who are regularly intended users for similar assignments; and*

- *what an appraiser's peers' actions would be in performing the same or a similar assignment.*

According to USPAP, **appraiser's peers** are defined as *other appraisers who have expertise and competency in a similar type of assignment.* For the scope of work to be acceptable, an appraiser expert witness must take steps to ensure that the scope of work meets or exceeds what would be expected by other parties in a similar court case and meets or exceeds what other expert witnesses would do in the same or similar court case. The comment continues to state:

- *If any investigation, information, method, or technique would appear relevant to the client, another intended user, or the appraiser's peers, an appraiser must be prepared to support the decision for its exclusion.*

The appraiser expert witness may be assured that opposing parties assessing the expert witness's scope of work will be looking for reasons to exclude anything in the development of the expert witness's opinions and conclusions.

Advisory Opinion 29 is specifically focused on guidance regarding the acceptability of the scope of work. In this excerpt from Advisory Opinion 29, the discussion of an "appraiser's peers" is helpful:

To be an appraiser's peer for a particular assignment, one must have the competency to address the appraisal problem presented in that assignment. This includes the knowledge and experience to:

- *properly identify the appraisal or appraisal review problem to be solved;*

- *determine the type and extent of research and analyses to include in the development process, and;*

- *perform the required research and analyses properly.*

The scope of work that was performed in an assignment must be disclosed in the report.

Disclosure Obligations

The final section of the SCOPE OF WORK RULE, <u>Disclosure Obligations</u>, presents a general disclosure obligation for the scope of work, plus a Comment that contains the rationale for the obligation and explanation of "sufficient information:"

The report must contain sufficient information to allow intended users to understand the scope of work performed.

<u>Comment</u>: *Proper disclosure is required because clients and other intended users rely on the assignment results.* **Sufficient information includes disclosure of research and analyses performed and might also include disclosure of research and analyses not performed.**

- **An appraiser must disclose research and analyses not performed when such disclosure is necessary for intended users to understand the report properly and not be misled.**

- These disclosure requirements apply to the scope of work performed, rather than the scope of work initially planned by the appraiser.

- There is no requirement for the scope of work description to be in a particular or separate section of the report.

Deficiency in the scope of work disclosure is one of the most frequently cited issues in general appraisal reporting, according to Fannie Mae, FHA, and many state regulators. For appraisals and appraisal review reports prepared for use in appraiser expert witness work, appropriate disclosure of the scope of work simply cannot be deficient.

Jurisdictional Exception Issues

Depending on the jurisdiction and the specific regulations being applied in a court proceeding, it might be possible that compliance with USPAP might be precluded due to laws or regulations applicable in an appraiser expert witness assignment. It is also quite possible that for an appraiser new to expert witness work, the appraiser has not had a circumstance for which the JURISDICTIONAL EXCEPTION RULE would be effective.

The JURISDICTIONAL EXCEPTION RULE is a provision of USPAP that applies whenever law or regulation of a jurisdiction **precludes compliance** with USPAP. Jurisdictional exception specifically applies to law or regulation that **takes away** from the force of that part of USPAP. Therefore, assignment conditions that add to the obligations of USPAP are not an example of a jurisdictional exception.

The JURISDICTIONAL EXCEPTION RULE includes obligations for an appraiser related to:

- Identification of the law or regulation that prevents full compliance with USPAP.

- Compliance with the particular law or regulation in performing the assignment.

- Disclosure requirements of the part of USPAP that is of no force due to the law or regulation.

- Citation of the law or regulation requiring a jurisdictional exception in the report.

The JURISDICTIONAL EXCEPTION RULE states, in part:

- *If any applicable law or regulation precludes compliance with any part of USPAP, only that part of USPAP becomes void for that assignment.*

When federal law or regulation requires compliance with USPAP, no part of USPAP can be voided by a state or local jurisdiction.

Law includes:

- Constitutions

- Legislative and court-made law

- Administrative rules and ordinances

Regulations include:

- Rules or orders having legal force and issued by an administrative agency

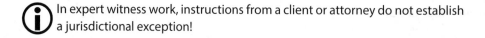 In expert witness work, instructions from a client or attorney do not establish a jurisdictional exception!

If the JURISDICTIONAL EXCEPTION RULE is applicable in an expert witness assignment, it is very important that the expert witness properly discloses its use. According to the JURISDICTIONAL EXCEPTION RULE:

In an assignment involving a jurisdictional exception, an appraiser must:

1. identify the law or regulation that precludes compliance with USPAP;

2. comply with that law or regulation;

3. ***clearly and conspicuously disclose in the report the part of USPAP that is voided by that law or regulation; and***

4. ***cite in the report the law or regulation requiring this exception to USPAP compliance.***

USPAP FAQs for JURISDICTIONAL EXCEPTION RULE

The USPAP FAQ's contain several applicable references to assist in understanding the applicability of the JURISDICTIONAL EXCEPTION RULE:

PROBATE COURT STATUTE BASING THE APPRAISAL FEE ON THE APPRAISED VALUE

Question: A property is being appraised for a probate court in a state which has a statute stipulating that appraisal fees for these assignments shall be based on the appraised value of the property. Does USPAP allow me to appraise the property under this compensation arrangement?

Response: Yes. This is an example where the JURISDICTIONAL EXCEPTION RULE applies. To comply with the requirements of the JURISDICTIONAL EXCEPTION RULE, the appraiser must disclose in the appraisal report the reason(s) that prohibit compliance with USPAP and cite the basis for the jurisdictional exception.

APPROPRIATE SOURCES FOR JURISDICTIONAL EXCEPTION

Question: My client's attorney has told me to invoke the JURISDICTIONAL EXCEPTION RULE to avoid mentioning in my appraisal report an underground storage tank (UST) that I know exists on the property. The attorney did not provide any reference or citation of law or regulation justifying this action. Can I follow the instruction from this attorney who is representing my client?

Response: No. Use of the JURISDICTIONAL EXCEPTION RULE is triggered by a conflict between the requirements of USPAP and the law or regulation of a jurisdiction, not by client discretion.

The JURISDICTIONAL EXCEPTION RULE states:

If any applicable law or regulation precludes compliance with any part of USPAP, only that part of USPAP becomes void for that assignment.

This Rule provides a saving or severability clause when compliance with a part or parts of USPAP is precluded by law or regulation. The first sentence of the Comment to the Rule states:

The JURISDICTIONAL EXCEPTION RULE provides a saving or severability clause intended to preserve the balance of USPAP if compliance with one or more of its parts is precluded by the law or regulation of a jurisdiction. When an appraiser properly follows this Rule in disregarding a part of USPAP, there is no violation of USPAP.

The second paragraph in the Comment also provides descriptions of laws and regulations that appraisers can use to determine when the use of the JURISDICTIONAL EXCEPTION RULE is acceptable. It is important to note that the parameters described in the Comment apply whether the assignment is an appraisal or appraisal review assignment, or the type and definition of value is market value or some other value opinion, and for any intended use.

An attorney's instruction, without specific citation of law or regulation, is not the equivalent of law or regulation. It is important to note the role of each:

- Attorneys may *offer legal opinions*
- Legislative bodies and courts *make laws*
- Administrative agencies *establish regulations*

While an attorney is an expert in the practice of law, it is the court that decides if the facts in a matter support an attorney's representation of how established law applies to a specific set of facts.

Absent the citation of law or regulation, which should be cited in the report together with the part or parts of USPAP from which compliance is precluded in the assignment, the attorney's instruction is not acceptable as a basis to disregard a part or parts of USPAP applicable in the assignment.

VALUATION METHODS AND JURISDICTIONAL EXCEPTION RULE

Question: I am doing an appraisal assignment for a government agency that is subject to the provisions of The Uniform Relocation Assistance and Real Property Acquisitions Act of 1970, as Amended (commonly known as, the Uniform Act), and its implementing regulation, 49 CFR Part 24. They have provided me with a reference to a State Court of Appeals ruling which indicates that standing timber and landscaping impacted by a public project must be appraised based on the value it contributes to the subject property as a whole, and not as individual items. They have informed me that this appeals case is frequently cited in condemnation cases and almost always upheld by trial courts in this state. Based on this court decision, the agency has adopted a policy that all standing timber and landscaping be valued in this manner.

On this issue of landscaping, does using contributory value versus replacement value constitute a jurisdictional exception?

Response: No. The JURISDICTIONAL EXCEPTION RULE does not apply in this circumstance since there are no requirements in USPAP addressing the proper valuation techniques for standing timber and landscaping. The Rule only applies when there is a conflict between the requirements of USPAP and the applicable law or regulation of a jurisdiction.

USPAP requires that in the development of an appraisal, an appraiser must be aware of, understand, and correctly employ those recognized methods and techniques that are necessary to produce a credible appraisal. Further, the COMPETENCY RULE requires recognition of, and compliance with, laws and regulations that apply to the appraiser or to the assignment.

The agency policy on the valuation of standing timber and landscaping is an assignment condition and must be considered in the scope of work decision. However, an appraiser cannot perform an assignment with a condition that would produce assignment results that are not credible in the context of the intended use.

Chapter Summary

1. Appraisers should be aware that they are obligated to adhere to **professional standards** when performing as a witness or as an expert witness.

2. Familiarity with **USPAP and its rules and standards** is a critical component of performing as a successful appraiser expert witness.

3. The appraiser has ethical responsibilities with regards to giving expert witness testimony, and the **Ethics Rule in USPAP** must be followed.

4. Appraisers must be familiar with the difference between **valuation services** and **appraisal practice** to understand their role in expert witness testimony assignments. Those engaged for their appraisal expertise are under the guidance of USPAP.

5. USPAP's **Conduct section in the Ethics Rule** dictates that the appraiser giving expert witness testimony must be impartial, objective, and independent, without accommodating personal interests. He must not advocate for any cause, including the cause promoted by the person who has engaged his services.

6. Parties engaging an appraiser expert witness for testimony need to be informed of any **current or prospective interest** in the subject property or of any **prior services** that took place within a three-year period preceding acceptance of an assignment; whether the witness was acting as an appraiser or in any other capacity.

7. The **Confidentiality Rule** in USPAP dictates that the appraiser keeps her client's information or assignment results confidential except for parties specifically authorized by the client, state appraiser regulatory agencies, third parties as may be authorized by due process of law, or a duly authorized peer review committee.

8. **Assignment results** are not simply the appraiser's opinion of value. They may include opinions or conclusions other than the value opinion. However, physical characteristics of a property are not assignment results.

9. The **Record Keeping Rule of USPAP** provides obligations for an appraiser regarding the appraiser's work file. An appraiser must prepare a work file for each appraisal assignment. It must be in existence prior to the issuance of any report.

10. An **oral report** requires that a written summary of the report be added to the work file within a reasonable time after the oral report is issued. A transcript of the appraiser's testimony fulfills this obligation.

11. Regarding **work file retention**, an appraiser must retain the work file for a period of at least five years after preparation or at least two years after final disposition of any judicial proceeding in which the appraiser provided testimony related to the assignment, which period expires last.

12. The **Scope of Work Rule in USPAP** applies when the appraiser is engaged to perform an appraisal or an appraisal review. When an appraiser is acting as a consultant, or in a similar role, and not performing an appraisal or appraisal review, there are no scope of work obligations.

13. **The appraiser** is charged with determining the scope of work with regards to an appraisal or an appraisal review assignment. Although an attorney or other engaging party may provide input for the scope of work decision, it is ultimately the appraiser's responsibility to ensure that any scope of work suggested by a client will produce credible assignment results.

14. The scope of work is acceptable when it **meets or exceeds** the expectations of parties who are regularly intended users for similar assignments, and what an appraiser's **peers' actions** would be in performing the same or a similar assignment.

15. **Jurisdictional exception** may or may not apply in a court proceeding. This rule discusses laws or regulations that preclude compliance with USPAP.

16. In some cases, an attorney in a case may direct the appraiser to invoke the Jurisdictional Exception Rule to avoid information being presented that does not advocate for their cause. **The appraiser** must determine whether the Jurisdictional Exception Rule applies.

Chapter Quiz

1. Assignment results, when part of an appraisal assignment which will result in expert witness testimony, must include
   A. the creation of a work file by the appraiser.
   B. an opinion of value.
   C. an opinion regarding another appraiser's work.
   D. the physical characteristics of a property.

2. Jurisdictional exception is an assignment condition that is established by the
   A. applicable law or regulation.
   B. appraiser.
   C. client.
   D. judge.

3. In an oral report, when no written report is part of the scope of work, a supporting work file
   A. can include a court transcript.
   B. is not required.
   C. must be created after testimony is complete.
   D. must include the appraisers' resume.

4. The difference between an appraisal assignment and a valuation service is that an appraisal assignment
   A. can be completed by a real estate agent.
   B. does not have Ethics Rule requirements.
   C. is outside of the scope of work.
   D. should comply with USPAP.

5. The Conduct Section of the Ethics Rule requires that an appraiser
   A. advocates for the cause of the party who engaged them.
   B. follows a scope or work dictated by their client.
   C. is impartial and objective.
   D. provides a valuation service outside of appraisal practice when providing testimony.

6. The appraiser must inform a client of any prior involvement regarding the subject property that took place within the prior
   A. 1 year.
   B. 2 years.
   C. 3 years.
   D. 5 years.

7. The Confidentiality Rule dictates that an appraiser must keep information or assignment results as confidential EXCEPT to
   A. anyone authorized by the client.
   B. anyone authorized by the client and any intended users.
   C. the judge or mediator in the case.
   D. local tax authorities.

8. The Jurisdictional Exception Rule is a provision of USPAP that applies whenever law or regulation of a jurisdiction _____ with USPAP.
   A. conflicts
   B. defaults
   C. performs alliance
   D. precludes compliance

9. An appraiser's work file must be retained for a period of at least _____ years after preparation, or at least _____ years after final disposition of any judicial proceeding in which the appraiser provided testimony related to the assignment, whichever period expires last.
   A. 3, 2
   B. 5, 1
   C. 5, 2
   D. 7, 3

10. There are no scope of work obligations when an appraiser is acting as a(n)
    A. appraiser.
    B. consultant.
    C. estimator.
    D. review appraiser.

Expert Witness in Practice

Key Terms

Client The party or parties who engage, by employment or contract, an appraiser in a specific assignment.

Confidential Information Information that is either 1) Identified by the client as confidential when providing it to an appraiser and is not available from any other source. 2) Classified as confidential or private by applicable law or regulation.

Extraordinary Assumption An assignment-specific assumption, directly related to a specific assignment, as of the effective date regarding uncertain information used in an analysis of the assignment results, which, if found to be false, could alter the appraiser's opinions or conclusions.

Hypothetical Condition A condition directly related to an assignment which is contrary to what is known by the appraiser to exist on the effective date of the assignment results but is used for the purpose of analysis.

Intended Use The use(s) of an appraiser's reported appraisal or appraisal review assignment results, as identified by the appraiser based on communication with the client at the time of the assignment.

Intended User The client and any other party as identified, by name or type, as users of the appraisal or appraisal review report by the appraiser, based on communication with the client at the time of the assignment.

Jurisdictional Exception An assignment condition established by applicable law or regulation which precludes an appraiser from complying with a part of USPAP.

Scope of Work The type and extent of research and analyses in an appraisal or appraisal review assignment.

Litigation Assignments versus Typical Appraisal Practice

Appraisers with substantial appraisal experience in their area of expertise may find the transition to expert witness work to be a challenge. Areas of focus for court work may be very different from their usual practice and require more preparation in specific areas. Understanding USPAP is essential for developing the competency and skills required to work as an expert witness.

Competency is the Key to Success

The ability to fully complete an assignment is the key to successful court work. Any lack of competency on the part of the appraiser will be glaringly obvious under the scrutiny of the hiring attorneys and those on the opposing side of a case. Identifying the key items and rules required to satisfy an assignment is the best line of defense for an appraiser to make sure he is prepared.

COMPETENCY RULE

An appraiser must; (1) be competent to perform the assignment; (2) acquire the necessary competency to perform the assignment; or (3) decline or withdraw from the assignment. In all cases, the appraiser must perform competently when completing the assignment.

Being Competent

The appraiser must determine, prior to accepting an assignment, that he or she can perform the assignment competently. Competency requires:

1. The ability to properly identify the problem to be addressed;

2. The knowledge and experience to complete the assignment competently; and

3. Recognition of, and compliance with, laws and regulations that apply to the appraiser or to the assignment.

Comment: Competency may apply to factors such as, but not limited to, an appraiser's familiarity with a specific type of property or asset, a market, a geographic area, an intended use, specific laws and regulations, or an analytical method. If such a factor is necessary for an appraiser to develop credible assignment results, the appraiser is responsible for having the competency to address that factor or for following the steps outlined below to satisfy this COMPETENCY RULE.

For assignments with retrospective opinion and conclusions, the appraiser must meet the requirements of this COMPETENCY RULE at the time of the assignment, rather than the effective date.

Acquiring Competency

If an appraiser determines he or she is not competent prior to accepting an assignment, the appraiser must:

1. Disclose the lack of knowledge and/or experience to the client before accepting the assignment;

2. Take all steps necessary or appropriate to complete the assignment competently; and

3. Describe, in the report, the lack of knowledge and/or experience and the steps taken to complete the assignment competently.

Comment: Competency can be acquired in many ways, including, but not limited to, personal study by the appraiser, association with an appraiser reasonably believed to have the necessary knowledge, and/or experience.

In an assignment where geographic competency is necessary, an appraiser who is not familiar with the relevant market characteristics must acquire an understanding necessary to produce credible assignment results for the specific property type and market involved.

When facts or conditions are discovered during an assignment that cause an appraiser to determine, at that time, that he or she lacks the required knowledge and experience to complete the assignment competently, the appraiser must:

1. Notify the client;

2. Take all steps necessary or appropriate to complete the assignment competently; and

3. Describe, in the report, the lack of knowledge and/or experience and the steps taken to complete the assignment competently.

Lack of Competency

If the assignment cannot be completed competently, the appraiser must decline or withdraw from the assignment.

Competency Rule #1 – Be Competent to Perform the Assignment

While it may seem like a simple rule to follow, appraisers often knowingly, and unknowingly, violate this rule in their normal course of business. The Competency Rule provides the appraiser with a framework for taking an assignment where he does not have competency. While a client may agree to allow the appraiser to take steps to complete the assignment, a court case is not a good place to acquire competency. An appraiser should be extremely careful when making the decision to take the expert witness assignment and he will need to establish clear direction and planning about how to acquire the missing knowledge.

Client Expectations

Clients often assume that any appraiser has the necessary knowledge to be a competent expert witness. It is the appraiser's responsibility to determine if her competency level is suitable to provide expert witness services for a particular case. Prior to the appraiser's engagement, she should ask detailed questions about the assignment to determine her suitability.

As stated in the Competency Rule:

Competency requires the ability to properly identify the problem to be addressed.

This requires that the appraiser, by questioning the client, determine the details of the assignment and scope of work required to compete the work.

Clients' Limited Knowledge of Licensing Requirements

A client may not be aware of the limits of an appraiser's licensing or certification. Rules vary by state, and the attorney engaging the appraiser as an expert witness may not be familiar with these limitations on assignment types. Prior to the appraiser accepting an assignment, it is wise to inform the attorney of these restrictions.

Incompetence Cannot Be Hidden

If an appraiser accepts an assignment for which he is not competent, the truth will likely surface in the courtroom. The appraiser must be transparent about his skills and abilities.

A lack of competency in the type of assignment or in a geographic area often becomes apparent during the detailed question-and-answer activities involved in a case. Case files are full of examples where an expert witness was proven to be inexperienced when delivering his testimony.

Competency Rule #2 – Acquire the Necessary Competency to Perform the Assignment

As you've learned, it is not advisable to acquire knowledge on the job in an assignment that involves expert witness testimony. Even when a client agrees it is acceptable for an appraiser to gain competence in the course of preparing the appraisal, a lack of significant knowledge and experience from prior similar work will be a weakness going forward.

However, this does not mean that an appraiser cannot perform more research or seek additional resources in the process of the assignment to gain more expertise in a specific area. For example, in preparation for the case, an appraiser might read a textbook or research case studies to gather more information that reinforces her existing knowledge.

Competency Rule #3 – Decline or Withdraw from the Assignment

Appraisers often overestimate their competency due to inflated confidence or in their efforts to increase business. Appraisers should not hesitate to decline assignments that are beyond their knowledge and experience.

Scope Creep in Litigation Work

It is not uncommon for an expert witness to accept an appraisal assignment for litigation purposes in which additional work is required that was not previously described. While the appraiser may have been well-qualified at the beginning of the assignment, steps must be taken by the appraiser to determine competency for newly added areas.

Scenario

Joan has accepted an appraisal assignment for a divorce case involving a residence on a country lot. Since she has appraised in this area for over 20 years and holds a residential appraisal license, she feels she is competent to complete the assignment. In fact, the client has engaged her in other assignments for similar purposes with success.

During her research for the appraisal, Joan discovers that a lot next door shares the same ownership as the residential parcel. Research shows this side lot with a barn is to be zoned Commercial. The client directs her to also appraise this parcel, as it was unknown to be a part of the proceedings at the start of the appraisal assignment.

As a licensed residential appraiser, Joan has two choices:

1. Appraise "outside the scope of her license". Even if this might be permitted in some jurisdictions, Joan has never appraised commercial parcels in her 20 years as an appraiser. She would have to explain her lack of competency to her client and ask him to agree to let her proceed as she takes proper steps to gain competency during the assignment.

2. Decline this portion of the assignment as she does not have the knowledge and experience to complete the assignment competently.

Declining Assignments based on Competency Limitations

When faced with a light workload and lack of income for a fee appraiser, it is sometimes a difficult decision to decline work that might solve those problems. However, the decision to decline work is a part of appraisal work. Recognizing one's limitations of knowledge and experience is an important asset in this field.

Gaining Competency as an Appraiser

How does an appraiser become "competent" and expand his skill set in other subject matter areas?

Specific direction for litigation work will be given later, but the following are some suggestions for an appraiser to gain competency in a new field:

- Decide on a new direction and begin taking courses, seminars, and workshops to gain expertise in that area. For example, if an appraiser decides that the goal is to appraise hotels and already has the correct licensing/certification towards that end but lacks competency, he could choose coursework in that subject matter *before* taking on such an appraisal assignment.

- Find a mentor in the desired area. For example, an appraiser lacking in commercial real estate experience could ask a commercial appraiser if he could accompany her on her next assignment, observe the research required, and review the report upon completion.

- Accept an appraisal assignment in this new subject matter, with a client's permission with regards to gaining competency during the assignment, that is not for litigation purposes. Work with a mentor to assist in completion of the assignment and for the purposes of review and guidance.

Once the appraiser has expanded his knowledge and experience into a new subject matter area and gained the required competency, he may then accept litigation work in that area.

Potential Conflicts of Interest

It is the obligation of the appraiser to inform the potential client of any possible conflicts of interest. Questions an appraiser can ask himself when considering the acceptance of an assignment may include:

- Have I appraised this property before? Disclosure as required by USPAP may apply.

- Will this prior appraisal result in a conflict of interest? Should I make the potential client aware of the prior appraisal? Disclosure as required by USPAP may apply.

- Have I appraised competing properties of the same type in the same market area that might result in a conflict of interest? Should I make the potential client aware of this possible conflict?

- Have I used any confidential data that would logically be used in this potential appraisal report that would result in a conflict of interest?

- Have I been engaged by any of the parties to the case as an appraiser or in any other capacity?

The client may not be aware of prior services or potentials for conflicts of interest. It is incumbent upon the appraiser to inform the client of any possible issues of which the client may not be aware.

Shift in Focus with Expert Witness Assignments

Depending on the type of the assignment, the appraiser may find that the appraisal report and subsequent testimony focus more on the research and analyses performed than on the final value conclusion. In this instance, the appraiser would be wise to extend his research and analysis beyond what is normally expected in other types of work.

As an expert witness, the appraiser should keep in mind that he will eventually be defending his work. Although one could argue that the appraiser defends his work in the normal course of business, the "on the spot" defense required during oral testimony can be intimidating unless the appraiser is properly prepared.

For example, he may want to include more detail than he might typically include when an assignment is for other purposes, such as:

- General data on the geographic area
- General data on the genre of property
- Specific data on the subject property's physical characteristics
- Specific detail on prior transfers of the subject property
- Research and analysis that resulted in the highest and best use determinations
- Sales or rental comparables or other data used
- Sales or rental comparables or other data that is not used
- Verification for data sources
- Exhibits to demonstrate data points in the courtroom

General Data in the Geographic Area

General data in the geographic area is a good example of a subject that might be a source of questions by attorneys. In their general questioning to determine competency, they might ask for details such as census counts, geographic boundaries, school district performance, recent changes in employment, new construction, infrastructure changes, etc.

An appraiser may find that the use of exhibits can be useful in describing a geographic area. This could be in the form of handouts, posters, or electronic presentations. This requires preparation before testimony, permission by the court or attorney for use, and practice in their use.

For Example

Let's say that the appraiser has an assignment of a home in an established subdivision with new construction taking place. What additional information might the appraiser provide that is above-and-beyond the research that would be done for a typical assignment? Consider the following:

- Number of homes already built in the subdivision
- Age range of homes
- Sales price range of homes
- Number of sales in the last year, last two years, etc.
- Number of new homes under construction
- Number of vacant lots remaining
- Sales price range of the vacant lots
- Quality of construction of new homes
- Cost range of new homes

Many of the items listed in the example are beyond what would normally be provided in a residential report yet might be requested during testimony. Geographic competency was already noted in the comment section of the Competency Rule and is essential in expert witness testimony. Possible exhibits for this example could include showing the borders of the subdivision, the school district boundaries, a list of sales, or an aerial view of the subdivision.

General Data on the Genre of the Property

General data on the genre of the property could include:

- Research for that specific property type on the number of sales in a larger geographic area other than the specific market area
- Research to determine typical size, features, and amenities
- Research on market trends

For Example

In a case involving a car wash facility, the appraiser might want to research and provide:

- The number of sales of car washes in the local area, the larger market, the state, or nationwide.
- The typical car wash facility: Number of bays, automatic versus self-serve, other profit centers in the facility such as vending machines or vacuums.
- A market analysis of the larger market with regards to increasing or decreasing values, new construction, profitability, etc.

It is easy to see that this research could be extensive or limited depending on the scope of work for the expected testimony.

Access to nationwide or regional databases and market trend summaries would be useful in developing this knowledgebase and could provide exhibits for use during a case. Of course, care should be given that permission is granted for use of any copyrighted material.

Specific Data on the Subject Property's Physical Characteristics

A residential observation for an appraisal for mortgage lending purposes might take anywhere from minutes to an hour; a residential observation for expert witness use could take much longer. The appraiser should be taking notes to secure more specific details.

For Example

An appraiser might ask an owner specific details regarding home components, such as:

- Age of roof and mechanical components
- Recent improvements and alterations
- Recent changes to the site
- Items in fair/poor condition requiring repair or further investigation

In this example, if a foundation were severely cracked and of concern for support of the home, the appraiser might ask an attorney to provide a foundation expert to provide an opinion of its suitability, cost to repair, etc. on which the appraiser could rely.

Sales History of the Subject Property

The appraiser may be questioned on the sales history of the subject property beyond normal USPAP requirements, such as the conditions of sale, reasons for transfer, etc. Research into circumstances of sale beyond what is typical would be a solid foundation for answering questions regarding questionable sale prices, exempt transfers, and types of transfers. Data sources could include public records, deeds of transfer, conveyance forms, and owners.

For example, questioning about sales history could involve:

- Prior sale prices that are substantially higher or lower than appraised value.
- Prior transfers that took place that involved partial interests.
- Prior transfers that involved atypical instruments such as quit claim deeds or land contracts.

Research and Analysis that Resulted in Highest and Best Use Determinations

Highest and best use is commonly discussed during expert witness testimony. Specific details regarding zoning, zoning changes, and allowable uses under a specific zoning classification would be significant in discussing the appraiser's conclusions regarding highest and best use decisions. Potential or proposed changes to zoning could be included in questions to an expert witness appraiser. An appraiser should be prepared to answer questions about the four tests of highest and best use for the property as vacant and as improved, which are:

- Legally possible
- Physically possible
- Financially feasible
- Maximally productive

Since highest and best use determinations can be a source of dispute in court cases, the appraiser's preparation with adequate research is imperative.

For Example

For example, questions about highest and best use could involve:

- Current zoning and allowable uses, or potential for zoning changes, which could impact what would be "legally possible"
- Current rules for new construction such as set-back requirements from lot lines, which could impact the ability for new construction to be "physically possible"
- Market trends of supply and demand, both for vacant lots and for improved properties, of the subject property's type, which could impact what is "financially feasible" and "maximally productive"

Sales or Rental Comparables or Other Data Used

The appraiser will likely be questioned on data specifics and report specifics. Often, on a real property report, questions will focus on hard data that may or may not have been fact-checked by another expert. It is imperative that the appraiser, when conducting research, provides hard data that is accurate. If inaccuracies are discovered during the research phase of a report, they should be detailed in the report rather than discovered during a case.

Often sales data, rental data, and other data specific to development of a value opinion is scrutinized.

For Example

For example, questions about comparable data could involve:

- Geographic boundaries chosen for the market area
- Sales data and any fact discrepancies
- Rental data and any fact discrepancies
- Prior sales data and any fact discrepancies
- Neighborhood price ranges, age ranges, etc.

Factual data, if found to be in error, is a foundation for calling into question the appraiser's competency. A double-check of facts and review by a second party are wise in preparation of these reports.

Sales or Rental Comparables or Other Data That is Not Used

The appraiser should be prepared to discuss other data that is offered upon cross-examination by the opposing counsel. In preparation of the appraiser's report, he could include in the report, or at least in his workfile, data on sales or rentals NOT used or other data discounted through further research.

For Example

For example, questions about unused data could involve:

- Why different geographic boundaries were not chosen
- Why other sales or rentals were not used

The appraiser can decline to discuss new data with which he is not familiar if it is offered during a case.

Verification of Data Sources

Since data discrepancies are not uncommon in court cases, it is imperative that the appraiser utilize all available verification sources.

In a typical appraisal for mortgage lending purposes, an appraiser might use public records and multiple listing data as data sources. When preparing for expert witness testimony, an appraiser could contact a buyer or seller, a REALTOR® involved with the sale, or local public officials with knowledge of the sale who could provide valuable information that could impact value. An appraiser who has gone the extra mile in securing data will appear competent when giving testimony.

For Example

For example, questioning could involve the data in the report regarding:

- Specific condition or quality of construction for the subject property.
- How data was obtained.
- Who provided data, including names and dates.
- Why data verification sources were not contacted.
- Why data was not available from a source.

An appraiser who is prepared to give reasonable answers on what data was available and from what source, why data was not available, and when or how it was provided will appear competent in the case.

Use of Exhibits

Exhibits can be helpful in showing evidence to courtroom participants. These can take several forms, depending on the case and the physical capabilities in the courtroom.

For Example

Examples may include:

- Dry-erase board or chalkboards
- Enlarged documents
- Drawings or sketches
- Graphs and charts
- Enlarged photographs
- Actual items
- Electronic presentations or videos

At the time of engagement, the appraiser should detail any exhibits with costs attached that might provide clearer testimony and include them as part of the engagement letter. Often, these exhibits are required to be delivered to the opposing counsel well before the court date.

Data that would serve as possible exhibits might include location maps, aerial maps, plat maps, flood maps, sketches of buildings, photographs of a subject property and/or comparable sales or rentals, graphs and charts showing market trends, and any data charts.

At the start of the assignment, the appraiser should ask the client for details regarding the physical environment of the courtroom and the preferred methods of exhibits. Often these exhibits will need to be prepared by professional printing companies and will need to be ordered ahead of a court date.

Taking on Expert Witness Work

Considering the complexity of litigation work and the knowledge and experience required for these assignments, why would an appraiser desire to take on work as an expert witness? Let's look at some reasons:

- It's a challenge
- It can be steady work that diversifies a client base
- It can be lucrative

There is no question about the challenge involved in being an expert witness, but if an appraiser has substantial knowledge and expertise, there is no reason that she cannot accept this new work. Many appraisers feel that providing expert witness services makes them better prepared in all assignments. A mind-shift to being ready to defend her appraisal work, which is part of providing this service, is an asset, no matter what the type of work being offered entails.

Many appraisers only take on fee appraisal work and many only for mortgage lending, with uncertain volume and an uncertain paycheck. Even in markets with declining appraisal volume, there is a steady demand for expert witnesses. People still get divorced, have legal disputes, and create estates when they die, whether the mortgage volume is high or low. All these create a constant demand for expert witness testimony.

Not only can these assignments diversify an appraiser's workload, they will allow him to be less dependent on the ebb and flow of mortgage lending volume. Assignments are often paid by the hour and can result in substantial income.

Finding Expert Witness Work

In Chapter 1, we discussed the types of cases that might involve expert witnesses. They included:

- Divorce
- Foreclosures
- Condemnation actions
- Environmental contamination
- Bankruptcy
- IRS matters
- Real estate taxation disputes
- Insurance disputes
- Appraisal and mortgage fraud
- Family and business matters
- Zoning
- Building defects and disputes

How does an appraiser find clients who are interested in providing him with expert witness work? Potential clients include:

- **Government Entities.** State and county governments have appraisal departments who hire staff appraisers or offer contracts to appraisers based on geographic expertise or expertise in a type of property. Often these assignments involve construction of highways or placement of easements, which might involve eminent domain proceedings. Becoming qualified for eminent domain work though state and federal departments can provide a steady stream of such assignments. Often, it requires some specific coursework for those interested in these assignments.

- **Courts.** Bankruptcy and other courts may have an "approved appraiser list" of those who have been accepted for such work. These could be at the state or local level. Contact with court officials can direct an appraiser to an application process.

- **Attorneys and Other Professionals**. Getting the word out to attorneys who routinely hire appraisers can be a means to securing expert witness work. Attorneys network with other attorneys and a recommendation by an attorney who had a successful case with an appraiser as expert witness may lead to future litigation assignments.

An initial contact by letter, with a resume attached, and with detail of areas of expertise (residential, commercial, type of property, or geographic areas) is a first step towards helping an appraiser offering this service.

Contacting professionals who are hired for estate planning, accounting, dissolution of marriages and partnerships, and other consultants can lead to assignments for litigation purposes.

Prepare for Testimony

As a beginner in expert witness testimony, there are several ways to prepare for delivery.

Seek Advice from Professionals

The following strategies may prove to be very helpful when preparing for testimony:

- **Establish a mentor.** Seeing another expert witness in action while giving court testimony will show an appraiser the physical setting for the trial and the flow of the proceedings. This may give him confidence in understanding the expectations of the judge and attorneys. If he is unable to find an expert who commonly gives testimony, an attorney may assist in locating expert witnesses, even if the expert is not an appraiser.

- **Work with an attorney.** An attorney who is willing to assist in preparing an appraiser for a role as an expert witness can provide important guidance. For example, they could role-play the question and answer session and give advice on expectations: Length of responses, when not to respond, the use of objections by attorneys, and other helpful courtroom procedures.

- **Review testimony from other cases.** An attorney may be willing to provide transcripts of other cases that included expert witness testimony. Reading the questions posed by attorneys and judges/mediators and reviewing the answers given can give the appraiser important hands-on knowledge of what will likely take place in a case.

- **Take on related work.** Providing testimony in board of revision cases, where the appraiser has been engaged to appraise property for county taxation purposes, can provide a lower stress environment for giving testimony. If the assignment is in a geographic area that the appraiser has substantial practice in, he may know the participants (county assessors, treasurers, attorneys, etc.), which may be a good beginning step.

Other positive scenarios with related work include:

- **Assignments of simplistic properties.** These assignments can also be a beginning step to providing these services. For example, a divorce case involving a residential property that is not complex might give the appraiser confidence in providing testimony.

- **Assignments in a geographic area that the appraiser knows best.** These assignments can add confidence in the appraiser's ability to answer questions.

Meet with the Hiring Attorney

Appraisers should ask for a face-to-face meeting with the attorney, or at least a phone call, to clarify the assignment. This can be an important part of the engagement process to ensure that the appraiser's expertise is sufficient for the assignment, that the time frame is clarified, and that compensation is discussed.

Subjects to discuss with the hiring attorney include:

- Required expertise
- The client and other intended users
- Dates for the report and for expected court presence
- Pre-trial meetings
- Pre-trial depositions
- Compensation expectations
- Transcript of depositions and testimony to satisfy USPAP workfile requirements
- Competing appraisals being produced by the opposing side
- Consultant's services, including:
  - Engineers
  - Environmental experts
  - Contractors
  - Home inspectors
  - Pest inspectors
  - Architects
  - Need for exhibits

Clarify Client and Intended Users

Clarification is necessary at the start of the assignment and is largely a confidentiality issue. With many parties involved in the litigation process, the appraiser must be very clear about who the client is, who the intended users are, and therefore who is entitled to information regarding the assignment.

The confidentiality rule in USPAP is applied here, providing guidance to appraisers regarding the sharing of information.

The Confidentiality Rule in USPAP states: *An appraiser must protect the confidential nature of the appraiser-client relationship.*

An appraiser must not disclose: (1) confidential information; or (2) assignment results to anyone other than:

- *The client*
- *Parties specifically authorized by the client;*
- *State appraiser regulatory agencies;*
- *Third parties as may be authorized by due process of law; or*
- *Duly authorized professional peer review committee except when such disclosure to a committee would violate applicable law or regulation.*

Once the client is established, it is important to determine if it is only the attorney who engages them or if it is also the attorney's client. Noting this detail is important as it clarifies who can receive communications of potentially confidential information going forward in the assignment.

An appraiser may be asked to violate confidentiality rules as the opposing parties may ask for information. During court testimony, the appraiser can look to the engaging attorney or the judge of the proceedings for clarification on what confidential information can be shared.

Discuss Compensation

Appraisers should not be hesitant to quote fees upfront to clarify the scope of work and resulting compensation. Many appraisers use a multi-tiered compensation arrangement, with several steps listed as more time is anticipated to be spent.

For example, a quote could include preparation of the appraisal report with additional charges for phone calls, email time, time spent at depositions and meetings, time spent at court and waiting for court, and travel time to and from meetings and the court proceedings. It could be a flat fee, or a flat fee plus hourly fees.

Since the assignment results are unknown, many appraisers receive a retainer or full fee at the beginning of the assignment, and if the outcome with regards to value will service the wishes of the client is also unknown.

Letters of Engagement

While many appraisers do not routinely provide an engagement letter or agreement for the client to sign, in these cases, it is standard to have a signed engagement letter to clarify fees, costs, and due dates as an expert witness.

The engagement letter clarifies that the appraisal services will meet all required standards of professional appraisal practice, with an understanding that the services will be objective and impartial. Details in a letter of engagement should include:

- Client(s) by name or type, and any intended users
- Due dates for a written report, if needed
- Clarification with regards to a written report versus an oral report, or both
- Details regarding the appraisal assignment
    - Identification of the subject property
    - Contact information for scheduling an observation
    - Level expected of the observation: Interior, exterior, or other information
    - Other documentation relevant to the assignment
- Scope of work expected, including specific details
- Effective date of the assignment results
- Other dates, such as deposition dates, court dates, and meeting dates
- Location of the court for testimony
- Compensation and date(s) due
- Agreement to provide transcripts of depositions and testimony after completion

- Explanation of any extraordinary assumptions or hypothetical conditions
- Statement with regards to professional standards to be followed
- Statement that services will be impartial and objective as required by professional standards
- Date of the engagement letter
- Signatures of all parties
- Effective date of the assignment may be retrospective, prospective, or another date

Litigation assignments often do not utilize the observation date as the effective date of the appraisal assignment. Rather, it may be a date of marriage, date of divorce, date of purchase, date of death of an owner, or other date. It may also involve more than one effective date, such as a "before" and "after" scenario. Clarification of this date is an integral part of the initial engagement and may affect the fee quote due to the apparent complexity of the assignment.

Accurate Resumes

Appraisers are expected to produce a detailed resume, including contact address and phone, education history, appraisal education and experience, related education and experience, documentation of licensing/certification, and documentation of any designations. Since this information can change over time, it is imperative that the appraiser review and update this document before submitting it to any parties to the litigation.

Urgent Appraisal Assignments

Attorneys and others who engage appraisers for litigation purposes may wait until the last minute, shortly before a court date, to engage an appraiser. They may have let the process progress with the assumption that a settlement would take place without incurring the cost to their client of an expert witness.

The appraiser is cautioned to only accept such assignments if there is enough time to credibly and competently complete the appraisal report and prepare for litigation. Mistakes are often made when last-minute assignments are accepted and become apparent during the litigation proceedings. Time to correctly complete the assignment is incumbent upon the appraiser.

Pre-Trial Meetings

Many attorneys supply an appraiser with their questions ahead of the trial and may want to rehearse potential answers in a meeting. This is not an attempt to direct the answers. The meeting is to prepare the appraiser for the direction of the testimony and specifics regarding what questions will be presented.

Another subject to discuss at a pre-trial conference is the documents an appraiser is expected to bring to the court hearing. Does the attorney want the appraiser to bring only the report? If so, she should bring a bound copy so that papers do not pull loose during the hearing. It is appropriate for the attorney to ask for the workfile and sometimes, the opposing attorneys will have already asked for a copy of the workfile as a part of the discovery process.

Anything that an appraiser brings to court is fair game for the opposing counsel to review. For example, items in a workfile may become exhibits during the proceedings. If mathematical calculations might be a part of the proceedings, it is wise for an appraiser to bring a calculator that she uses regularly, if it is needed.

Testimony Proceedings and Expectations

Understanding what information will be expected, how it should be delivered, and the sequence of events that will unfold in the testimony of an expert witness is important.

Qualifying as an Expert Witness

The testimony will start with qualifying the appraiser as an expert witness. Questioning may focus on general knowledge of the area. It is common, in this case, to be asked how many appraisal reports have been prepared in that specific geographic territory over a recent time period. As part of the appraiser's preparation for testimony, it is wise to have that information available and accurate.

Scenario

ATTORNEY: Mr. Appraiser, how long have you been appraising in X county?

APPRAISER: I have been appraising full-time in X county for the last five years.

ATTORNEY: And how many appraisal reports have you prepared in that county over that period of time?

APPRAISER: I have prepared over 100 appraisals.

This is part of the attorney's attempt to prove that the appraiser they engaged for the assignment is qualified to be an expert witness. Geographic competency is a large part of this qualification and has already been discussed. USPAP comments regarding geographic competency are an important reminder to the appraiser to accept assignments in areas in which he is familiar.

Other pre-qualifying questions that are commonly asked, depending on the type of court proceedings involved, include:

- Home address and business address
- Typical appraisal territory
- Number of appraisals in a certain territory
- Type of appraisals prepared in a certain territory over a specified period of time
- Level of licensing or certification
- Professional designations or honors
- Past clients for court proceedings
- Names of jurisdictions (courts) where testimony took place

Restrict Answers to the Cover the Question

Legal experts often advise that witnesses only respond to the question asked. If a question only needs a "yes" or a "no" answer in response, that is the only answer is required. If such a response might mislead the attendees, a longer response could be given.

Scenario 1

ATTORNEY: How long were you at the subject property for your inspection?

APPRAISER: The observation took approximately 20 minutes.

ATTORNEY: Only 20 minutes?

APPRAISER: Yes.

Responding in this way could lead the observers to believe that 20 minutes for an observation was not enough and that the appraiser was not diligent in his observation.

Scenario 2

ATTORNEY: How long were you at the subject property for your inspection?

APPRAISER: The observation took approximately 20 minutes.

ATTORNEY: Only 20 minutes?

APPRAISER: Yes, 20 minutes was an adequate period of time for me to complete the observation, as the home was small and all on one floor. That is a typical time frame for residential appraisers in my office, based upon the assignment conditions.

The second scenario leaves a more desirable impression on the attendees that the appraiser has performed services in a "typical' fashion" as her peers would perform the same services.

The attorney who has engaged an appraiser can guide them through her testimony to ensure inclusion of all the points necessary for a complete understanding of the appraisal process and results. If a cross-examination leads to a confusing or unclear point, the attorney can re-direct questions after cross-examination to clarify those points.

Emphasize the Research and Analyses

Testimony may focus more on the research and the analyses processes than on the assignment results. The benefit to an attorney of employing an appraiser as an expert witness can be that the appraiser has wide ranging knowledge. Her range of appraisal experience with regards to information on a specific geographic area, general market conditions surrounding the appraisal assignment, or a comparison of the subject property to other properties' physical features is very useful. To highlight this extended knowledge, the attorney may concentrate questioning on the research and analyses she performed in the assignment.

For a fee appraiser who is used to a client's focus on value, especially when preparing appraisals for mortgage lending, this may be a surprise and require more preparation and focus on the appraiser's part with regards to research on general data rather than specific data. This can prove to be a difficult shift for the appraiser who is just beginning to take on work as an expert witness.

Appraisal Process Summary

A step-by-step summary of the appraisal process may be required. Attorneys will routinely guide the appraiser through a question-and-answer session about the steps in the appraisal process. Answering these questions can be made easier by including a flow chart of the appraisal process as a part of the appraisal report, since the court participants may not be familiar with the steps in the process. Also, this can be produced as an exhibit to facilitate understanding.

In the case of a jury trial, it is especially important for the appraiser to use layman's terms to provide clarity in the description of the appraisal process. Using technical terms may result in confusion and misconceptions in a court case.

Limit Testimony to the Assignment

It is not unusual for testimony to start with discussion of the specific appraisal, and then lead into other subjects that may not be in the appraiser's area of expertise. An appraiser may need to decline to comment when the questions posed by attorneys do not relate to her knowledgebase, license, or certification.

Scenario

ATTORNEY: Ms. Appraiser, tell the court about agricultural values in this area.

APPRAISER: I am not an agricultural appraiser; I appraise residences within the limits of my license in this state.

ATTORNEY: Certainly, you have heard what agricultural values are in this area as you have appraised nearby houses?

APPRAISER: I do not have specific knowledge regarding agricultural values in this area as that is not within the scope of my appraisal license and work.

An appraiser does NOT have to answer every question. The engaging attorney may provide an *objection* to this type of questioning; they will not want to offer unfounded opinions and be proven incompetent on a new, unexpected subject.

Clarify Extraordinary Assumptions or Hypothetical Conditions

Appraisal assignments for litigation purposes may include the need for extraordinary assumptions or hypothetical conditions. Let's review their definitions:

Extraordinary Assumption:

An assignment-specific assumption as of the effective date regarding uncertain information used in an analysis which, if found to be false, could alter the appraiser's opinions or conclusions.

> *Comment: Uncertain information might include physical, legal, or economic characteristics of the subject property; or conditions external to the property, such as market conditions or trends; or the integrity of data used in an analysis.*

> *Hypothetical Condition:*
>
> *A condition, directly related to a specific assignment, which is contrary to what is known by the appraiser to exist on the effective date of the assignment results but is used for analysis.*
>
> > *Comment: Hypothetical conditions are contrary to known facts about physical, legal, or economic characteristics of the subject property; or about conditions external to the property, such as market conditions or trends; or about the integrity of data used in an analysis.*

Clarification at the time of the engagement of the appraiser with regards to the need or use of extraordinary assumptions or hypothetical conditions in a litigation assignment is imperative.

Long and Unclear Questions

An appraiser may be asked a question that is unclear. It could be a very long question, with several questions within a question. A good technique to employ, in this scenario, is to ask the attorney to ask the question again. If it still unclear, an appraiser can say that he needs the question clarified. This does not make the appraiser appear incompetent if it is appropriately handled. It can make the appraiser appear diligent and concerned that he is providing the proper answer.

Appraisal Expert Witness Role

Appraiser witnesses must always be impartial. It can be very easy for the appraiser expert witness to become wrapped up in doing a good job for the engaging party's side and gravitate toward partiality. Unless the appraiser is vigilant of this obligation, he or she can be easily led toward the interests of the engaging party by the engaging side's attorney."

Other expert witnesses are permitted to be advocates; it may even be a requirement. This may lead to the appraiser being misled to believe that this is his role. The attorney could try to lead the appraiser during preparation of the report or during testimony as the attorney is an advocate for her client's interest. The appraiser must be careful to not imply that he is promoting or advocating for the attorney's client.

Another pitfall can occur if the attorney who is engaging the appraiser asks the appraiser to ignore certain facts without disclosure; in some cases, the attorney will argue "jurisdictional exception" as previously stated in Chapter 1. It is the appraiser's obligation to follow ethical guidelines and rules to appropriately include all relevant information. Lack of sufficient disclosure could result in a misleading report.

Case Appearance

Typically, expert witnesses are only called for their testimony and are not allowed to watch the proceedings so that their experience does not influence their testimony. Exceptions to this rule may exist in particular circumstances.

As you've learned, most cases settle prior to an actual court case. However, this may happen at the last minute, with all parties gathered at the courthouse. An agreement with the hiring entity should include compensation that includes: Any meetings and phone calls, including pre-trial; depositions and preparation for depositions; travel time to and from meetings and court; and court time/waiting for court time. Many appraisers quote hourly rates plus an appraisal report cost, since predicting the scope of the assignment up-front may be difficult.

An appraiser must always be prepared to deliver his expert witness testimony and not assume that the case will settle before testimony is given.

Request a Transcript

Appraisers should ask for a copy of the transcript of any depositions and testimony to satisfy USPAP workfile requirements when the process concludes. There is often a delay in production of transcripts of testimony. Remind the parties involved that part of the contract included receipt of any transcripts. Transcripts can be several dollars per page; include this requirement as part of the contract and be sure they are received.

Review Another Appraiser's Work Product

The assignment may include a review of another appraiser's work, or may be the only assignment. As part of litigation proceedings, attorneys and consultants routinely hire appraisers to review another appraiser's work. They may be looking for weaknesses in another's appraisal report to prepare a strong case for court. They may consider the review as a basis for deciding whether to enter an appraisal report as evidence.

As previously stated, it is necessary for the appraiser to follow USPAP Standard Rule 3 in taking on such a review assignment. This is not a role with bias against another's work; rather, it is an assignment to impartially and objectively complete a review of another's work. This review may or may not involve a development of an opinion of value by the reviewer; this should be clarified with the client at the time of engagement.

Establish Markers of Success

The appraiser must gain an understanding of the success of the assignment. There is not a "win" or a "loss" in the case, since the appraiser does not represent or advocate for a side. Rather, a successful assignment involving expert witness testimony involves the production of a detailed and defensible appraisal report, clear and concise testimony, and ability to defend the appraisal in court. That success will lead to other assignments and continued success as an expert witness in appraisal.

Chapter Summary

1. Appraisers should be aware that there are **challenges they will face** in transitioning from fee work to expert witness work, with different preparation and focus.

2. The appraiser must be familiar with **the Competency Rule in USPAP**, to accept or reject work assignments within his competency level. This includes having adequate knowledge and experience to complete the assignment. Geographic competency is included, as well as competency regarding assignment type.

3. An appraiser's client may not be familiar with the appraiser's level of expertise and may make assumptions that the assignment can be competently completed. **The burden is on the appraiser** to ascertain the nature of the assignment to determine if she is already competent.

4. The Competency Rule includes a section detailing **how to obtain the adequate competency during the assignment** if the appraiser does not already possess such competency.

5. **Scope creep** can be a consideration in litigation work, which consists of additional requests from the client than were in the original agreement.

6. Appraisers must avoid potential **conflicts of interest**, such as having prepared prior appraisals, or prior relationships with parties involved in the litigation.

7. Those accepting expert witness assignments should be prepared to provide **more factual detail** for potential testimony than in other types of appraisal assignments.

8. **Reasons appraisers take on litigation assignments** that may lead to expert witness testimony could include the desire for a challenge, economic gain, and diversification of client base.

9. **Possible clients** who need the services of an appraiser for litigation assignments can include government entities, the courts, and attorneys and other professionals.

10. **Training and preparation for testimony** can include working with a mentor, working with an attorney, reviewing testimony from other cases, or taking on related work.

11. Information that the appraiser will be required to **prepare for a litigation assignment** includes clarification of the client and intended users, discussion of compensation, preparation of a letter of engagement to be signed by all parties, and updating of the appraiser's resume. Having a meeting or call with the client before a trial begins enables the appraiser to be more adequately prepared for giving testimony.

12. An **appraiser's qualifications** will be determined at the start of his testimony, to ascertain his competency to complete the assignment. This may include questions regarding the number of appraisals prepared in a specific geographic area or regarding level of licensing and professional designations.

13. An appraiser's testimony may focus more on **research and analyses processes** than on the assignment results.

14. **Extraordinary assumptions** or **hypothetical conditions** must be clarified if they are part of the assignment.